CAMDEN MARKET 6

Arbeitsheft Inklusion

Erarbeitet von
Gisela Ehlers und Christina Wolkenhauer

unter Mitwirkung der Redaktion
Daniel Walker

Herausgeber der bisherigen Reihe
und Berater der Programmleitung:
Otfried Börner, StD a.D.,
Dr. phil. h.c. Christoph Edelhoff, StD a.D.

Diesterweg
westermann

CAMDEN MARKET 6

Materialien für Schülerinnen und Schüler
- Workbook 6 mit Audio-CD
  (ISBN 978-3-425-**73826**-0)
- Kit 6 (ISBN 978-3-425-**73846**-8)
- Westermann Vokabeltrainer-App
  www.westermann.de/vokabeltrainer

Materialien für Lehrkräfte
- Lehrerfassung zum Textbook 6 (ISBN 978-3-425-**73986**-1)
- Workbook 6 mit Lösungen und Audio-CD
  (ISBN 978-3-425-**73816**-1)
- Teacher's Manual mit Lösungen 6 (ISBN 978-3-425-**73866**-6)
- Vorschläge für Lernerfolgskontrollen 6
  (ISBN 978-3-425-**73916**-8)
- Audio-CD + DVD 6 für Lehrkräfte (ISBN 978-3-425-**73856**-7)
- Differenzierende Kopiervorlagen 6 (ISBN 978-3-425-**73876**-5)

Vorbereiten. Organisieren. Durchführen.
BiBox ist das umfassende Digitalpaket zu diesem Lehrwerk
mit zahlreichen Materialien und dem digitalen Schulbuch.
Für Lehrkräfte und für Schülerinnen und Schüler sind verschiedene Lizenzen verfügbar. Nähere Informationen unter
www.bibox.schule

© 2018 Bildungshaus Schulbuchverlage Westermann Schroedel Diesterweg Schöningh Winklers GmbH,
Georg-Westermann-Allee 66, 38104 Braunschweig
www.westermann.de

Druck A³ / Jahr 2023
Alle Drucke der Serie A sind im Unterricht parallel verwendbar.

Redaktion: Daniel Walker
Layout: Druckreif! Sandra Grünberg, Braunschweig
Illustrationen: Ulf Marckwort, Kassel
Umschlaggestaltung: blum design und kommunikation, Hamburg
Druck und Bindung: Westermann Druck Zwickau GmbH, Crimmitschauer Straße 43, 08058 Zwickau

ISBN 978-3-425-**73786**-7

Welcome!

Liebe Schülerinnen und Schüler,

das *Camden Market Arbeitsheft Inklusion 6* bereitet euch in diesem Jahr gezielt auf den Endspurt vor.

Zu Beginn werdet ihr euch mit den Herausforderungen des Erwachsenwerdens beschäftigen und dabei auch einiges über Nordirland erfahren.

Anschließend könnt ihr euch über eure Zukunftspläne, auch beruflicher Art, austauschen und ihr nehmt das Thema Kinderarbeit unter die Lupe.

Danach werdet ihr auf eine Reise nach Südafrika gehen. In der Regenbogen-Nation gibt es unglaublich viel zu entdecken.

Nicht weniger spannend dürfte es schließlich beim Thema Naturkatastrophen zugehen sowie bei der Beschäftigung mit dem Smartphone, sozialen Netzwerken und Co.

In *Theme* 5 (*Exam Practice*) könnt ihr euch schließlich mit den verschiedenen Aufgabenformaten der Abschlussprüfung vertraut machen.

Und jetzt: Viel Spaß mit dem *Camden Market Arbeitsheft Inklusion 6*!

Camden Market Arbeitsheft Inklusion 6

Mit diesem Rätsel kannst du den sechsten Band vom Arbeitsheft Inklusion
kennen lernen und dein Wissen über viele interessante Themen, die in deinem
Heft vorkommen, testen. Dazu musst du ein bisschen blättern.
Vor jeder Antwortmöglichkeit steht ein Buchstabe.
Kreise immer den richtigen Buchstaben ein.
Du erhältst dann einen Lösungssatz.

1 Auf Seite 11 findest du das
Inhaltsverzeichnis.
Welches _Theme_ beginnt auf Seite 57?
(T)   Growing up
(S)   Changes and challenges

2 Auf Seite 51 liest du
über Nelson Mandela.
Wo kommt er her?
(T)   Südafrika
(S)   Großbritannien

3 Auf Seite 46 findest du eine
Seite aus einem
Kapstadt-Reiseführer.
**Welche Sehenswürdigkeit wird
ganz unten beschrieben?**
(H)   Robben Island
(E)   Table Mountain

4 Auf Seite 15 lernst du zwei Teenager
aus Nordirland kennen.
Wie heißen sie?
(A)   Kevin und Sadie
(O)   Kevin und Sarah

5 **Wofür ist die Warnung auf Seite 62?**
(L)   Erdbeben
(R)   Tornados

Falls du nicht alles lösen kannst, versuche es am Ende des Schuljahres noch einmal.

6 Welche Farbe findest du auf der südafrikanischen Flagge?
(E)   Lila
(I)   Schwarz

7 Welche Stadt befindet sich in Südafrika?
(B)   New York
(C)   Kapstadt

8 Was ist das Thema des 5. Kapitels?
(R)   Exam practice
(F)   Natural disasters

9 Worum geht es im Text auf den Seiten 92 und 93?
(I)   ein billiges T-Shirt
(U)   einen schönen Mantel

10 Was kannst du auf Seite 41 selber gestalten?
(E)   eine Kappe
(N)   ein T-Shirt

11 Worum geht es im Text auf Seite 69?
(T)   Future plans
(W)   How to stay safe online

_ O U _ _ _ F _ _ _ A _ –
1   2 3 4   5 6 7

T H E _ _ A _ _ B O _ _ N A T I O N
       8   9 10   11

Hast du das Rätsel gelöst? Super!

Viel Spaß im neuen Schuljahr!

1 Teenagers in Europe

a) **Listen and read along.**

1
p. 4

1–3

Sophie, 16

I am visiting Oxford with my hip hop club. We are from Leiden in the Netherlands. We are performing at the *Dancin' Oxford* festival because Oxford is our twin town. English people are well-known for having unhealthy food. But my host family eats lots of fruit, vegetables and salad.

Hello, I am visiting Oxford with my football team from Bonn in Germany. Oxford is our twin town. We played a few matches against the local team. We all thought that the English would be very polite, but during the match they shouted and cheered like us. I get on really well with the English team, and we have had lots of fun.

Marcel, 17

Marika, 17

I live in Gdansk in Poland, and I am doing a language course here in Oxford. When I leave school, I would like to find a job in England, so I need to practise my English. I am staying in a youth hostel together with the other members of my course. I was surprised to find out that the English don't drink tea all the time! And they don't eat sausages and eggs for breakfast every day.

b) Underline important information about each person.
Find out about:

1. name and age un ✏

2. where he / she is from   un ✏

3. reason for visiting Oxford   un ✏

 c) Fill in the missing information.

name	age	country	reason for visiting Oxford
Sophie	___	the ___ Netherlands	performing at the Dancin' Oxford festival with her hip hop club
___	___	___	___
___	___	___	___

d) Work with a partner. Choose one of the teenagers. Talk about him / her.
Use your grid from c) for help.

> Sophie / Marcel is ...

> He / She came to Oxford
> because he / she is ...

> He / She is from ...

D

2 Typical British?

3
p. 5

a) Look at the cartoon. Then find the matching sentence. Tick.

☐ English people always drink tea.

☐ English people are very polite.

☐ English people love to talk about the weather.

 b) Read the texts in number 1 again. Underline what the teenagers thought about the English before their visit. un

 c) Put the words in the right order.

Sophie thought – unhealthy food. – English – only – people – eat

_____

Marcel thought – people – very – are – English – polite.

_____

Marika thought – tea. – people – drink – always – English

_____

3 Typical German?

a) What do people say is typical about Germans? Listen and circle.

They are very serious.

They drink beer.

They wear lederhosen.

They eat fish.

They eat sausages.

They are on time.

 b) What do <u>you</u> think? Talk to a partner.

I think it's right.
Germans often ...

I think it's wrong.
Not all Germans ...

4 Travelling to Oxford

a) Listen and number.

 **b) Listen again. Is it true or false?**

	true	false
1. The train will be two hours late.		
2. There are no buses going to Aviemore today.		
3. Sandra is looking for her father.		

.5 At Cologne station

6
p. 6

a) Read the timetable.

Abfahrt Departure   DB

Zeit		Über		Nach	Gleis	
14:45	RE 29723	Dormagen •	Neuss	KREFELD Hbf	9	
14:47	RE 4868	Düren •		AACHEN Hbf	8	ca. 5 Minuten später
14:48	ICE 124	Duisburg •	Oberhausen	AMSTERDAM CENTRAAL	5	ca. 10 Minuten später
14:49	ICE 651	Wuppertal •	Hannover	BERLIN Hbf	2	
14:51	RE 10125	Köln Messe/Deutz •	Duisburg • Dortmund	HAMM (Westf)	4	Zug fällt aus
14:52	ICE 14	Siegburg/Bonn •	Frankfurt (M) Flughafen Fernbf	FRANKFURT (MAIN) Hbf	3	
14:53	IC 2115	Bonn • Koblenz •	Heidelberg	STUTTGART Hbf	7	
14:54	ICE 509	Mannheim •	Karlsruhe • Freiburg	BASEL SBB	6	Zug wird geteilt
15:01	RB 12573	Köln Messe/Deutz •	Troisdorf	KOBLENZ	3	

b) Answer the questions in English. Work with a partner.

> 1. Which train goes to Heidelberg?

> 2. When is the next train to Freiburg?

> 3. Is the train to Oberhausen on time?

> 4. From which platform does the train to Hanover leave?

Land und Leute

Die Europäische Union startete mit einem Wirtschaftsabkommen zwischen sechs europäischen Ländern. Sie wollten enger zusammenarbeiten, um sicher zu sein, dass sich so etwas Schreckliches wie der 2. Weltkrieg nie wiederholen würde. Diese sechs Länder waren: Deutschland, Frankreich, Italien, die Niederlande, Belgien und Luxemburg.

Seitdem erinnert man mit dem Europatag am 9. Mai an den Tag, an dem dieses Abkommen zur Schaffung des vereinten Europas im Jahre 1950 diskutiert wurde.

Inhalt

Symbole und Verweise

Diese Dinge übst du:

 Hören

 Sprechen

 Wortschatz

 Lesen

 Schreiben

 Hier kannst du auf Deutsch z. B. über englische Schilder sprechen.

 Dieser Text ist auf CD.
1–3

 Diese Aufgabe ist ein bisschen schwieriger.

 Hier gibt es eine thematisch passende Aufgabe im
1
p. 18
Camden Market Textbook.
Die obere Zahl nennt die Aufgabennummer,
die untere die Seitenzahl.

Wörter in grauer Schrift kannst du in deinen eigenen Sätzen austauschen.

Diese Kästen werden dir im Buch begegnen:

 Hier findest du wichtige Redemittel.

 Hier findest du Tipps zum Englischlernen.

 Hier bekommst du Tipps zu den Aufgaben.

Growing up

In diesem *Theme* ...

- liest du über ein junges Paar und ihre Probleme.
- erfährst du etwas über die Vergangenheit Irlands und Nordirlands.
- beschäftigst du dich mit einem Film über einen schwangeren Teenager.
- sprichst du über die Rollen in einer Beziehung.
- erstellst du ein Filmposter.

1 At the bus stop

a) Look at the photo.
What are the teenagers thinking about?

> James **is thinking about …**

b) Listen to the teenagers.

c) Match the sentence parts.

1. James is thinking about   school problems.

2. Sam is thinking about   first love.

3. Olivia is thinking about   problems with his parents.

4. Alex is thinking about   problems with her brother.

d) Read out the sentences in class.

2 Kevin and Sadie

2
p. 18

a) Describe the teenagers.

18 years old

Belfast, Northern Ireland

16 years old

eight brothers and sisters

one brother

an unskilled worker

Kevin McCoy

Sadie Jackson

a shop assistant

The name of the boy is ...
He is ... / He has ...

The name of the girl is ...
She is ... / She has ...

b) This is a text about the teenagers in the book *Across the Barricades*. Listen and read along.

7

Du musst nicht jedes Wort verstehen. Versuche nur den Inhalt zu erschließen.

Sadie has spent the afternoon with Kevin. She now returns home.

[...] Sadie stood with her head up listening to her mother's tirade[1]. At the end of it she said, "All I've done is go for a walk
5 with a boy."
"All?" said her mother.
"You're not seeing him again, do you hear?" said her father.
"I'll see him if I want to."
10 Sadie opened the kitchen door.
"Come you back here," roared[2] her father. [...] "You'll do what I tell you as long as you're

living under my roof[3]." 15
"I don't have to stay under your roof. I'm sixteen, going on seventeen. I can go if I want to. You can't get the police to bring me back." 20
[...] Sadie [...] walked up the stairs. He made to follow her but his wife said quietly, "Let her be, Jim." [...]

---

[1] tirade – Geschimpfe
[2] roared – brüllte
[3] Dach – roof

c) Look at number 1 again. What is Sadie's problem? Talk to a partner.

She has problems with ...

Land und Leute

Im Jahr 1800 wurde Irland zu einem Teil des Vereinigten Königreichs gemacht. 1948 spaltete sich der südliche Teil Irlands ab und bildete die Republik Irland. Nordirland blieb Teil des Vereinigten Königreichs. Die *Nationalisten* in Nordirland aber, die überwiegend Katholiken waren, wollten auch Teil der Republik Irland werden. Die überwiegend protestantischen *Unionisten* hingegen wollten lieber zum Königreich gehören. Mit Beginn der siebziger Jahre wurden die Auseinandersetzungen zwischen den beiden Gruppen immer gewalttätiger. 1998 kam es unter der Leitung der britischen Regierung zu Friedensverhandlungen mit allen unterschiedlichen Gruppierungen. Alle stimmten einer friedlichen Lösung zu. Bis heute herrscht Misstrauen und manchmal kommt es noch zu gewaltsamen Übergriffen zwischen den katholischen und protestantischen Gruppen.

3 The story goes on

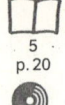

5
p. 20

8

a) **Look at the pictures. Listen and point.**

> Schau dir zuerst die Bilder genau an. Dann suche beim Zuhören nach einem Schlüsselwort, das zum Bild passt.

b) Read and match the sentences and the pictures.

1. Kevin arrives at the river. He waits for Sadie.

2. An old man, Mr Blake, helps Kevin.

3. Sadie arrives at the river and sees Kevin and Mr Blake.

4. Kevin and Sadie start seeing each other at Mr Blake's place.

5. Sadie loses her job. She becomes Mr Blake's housekeeper.

6. Someone throws a bomb into Mr Blake's house.

4 Kevin's plans

6
p. 20

9

a) Listen to Kevin. What are his plans? Circle.

> I'm going to stay. It's safer for me here.

> I want to go away. I can't stay here any longer.

doesn't have a job •
is sick of bombs •
is sick of people getting killed • ...

b) Listen again. Write down one reason for his plans.

Kevin wants to ... _____

because ... _____

_____

5 How the story ends

7
p. 21

a) **Look at the pictures. What can you see?**

b) **Underline the correct words.**

1. Kevin saw Sadie / his mother at the harbour.

2. She showed Kevin her bag / ticket.

3. They left Northern Ireland / Wales and went to Liverpool.

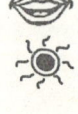

c) **Do you think this is a happy ending? Why? Talk to a partner.**

6 A dialogue

8
p. 21

Work with a partner. Present a dialogue between Kevin and his mum in class.

> Die Dialogteile findest du bei Aufgabe I im Anhang.

1. Cut out the pieces of dialogue.

2. Put them in the correct order and glue them onto the next page.

3. Choose a role and practise the dialogue with your partner.

4. Present the dialogue in class.

7 Juno

a) **Read the notes. Write sentences about the girl.**

9
p. 22

> Name: Juno MacGuff
> Age: 16
> Boyfriend: Paulie Bleeker
> Other information: pregnant

1. She is called _____.

2. She is _____.

3. Her boyfriend _____.

4. She is _____.

8 The story

10/12
p. 23/24
10

a) **Listen and read along.**

> Du kannst unbekannte Wörter in einem Wörterbuch oder hinten in deinem Buch nachschlagen.

Juno

It is another boring afternoon.
16-year-old Juno meets with Paulie.
She sleeps with him to see what it is like.
Then she is pregnant.
She knows that she does not want to keep the baby.
She decides not to have an abortion.
Juno gives up her baby for adoption.
Together with her best friend Leah, Juno looks for a family for her baby.

b) Read the questions.
Then underline the answers in the article.

1. Who does Juno meet on a boring afternoon?

2. What happens to Juno? un

3. What does Juno decide to do with her baby? un

4. Who helps Juno find a family for her baby? un

 c) Check with your partner.

 d) What do you think of the ending? Is it happy or sad?
Talk to your partner.

> I think the ending is happy.
> Juno and Paulie fall in love.

> I think the ending is sad, because
> Juno gives her baby away ...

9 Scenes

p. 22/23

Look at the pictures.
They show scenes from the film *Juno*.
Choose two and describe them to your partner.

> In picture A I can see
> Juno. She is with ...

A

B

C

D

10   Family life

Look at the picture.
What are the people doing?
Talk to your partner.

cooking • cleaning •
coming home from work • hoovering •
looking after the baby • ...

The man is ...

The woman is ...

11   On the radio

14/15
p. 23/24

11

a) Listen. What is Tom talking about?

Tom is talking about ...

family life.   school life.

b) Listen again. Circle the correct word.

1. Tom's wife is a teacher / doctor.

2. Tom is an author / actor. He works in an office / from home.

3. Tom can spend a lot of time with his children / dog.

c) Talk to your partner.
Tell him / her about Tom's life in German.

Tom arbeitet als ...

12 **Jobs at home**

15
p. 25

a) **Look at the statistics about jobs at home in marriages.**
   Then complete the sentences.

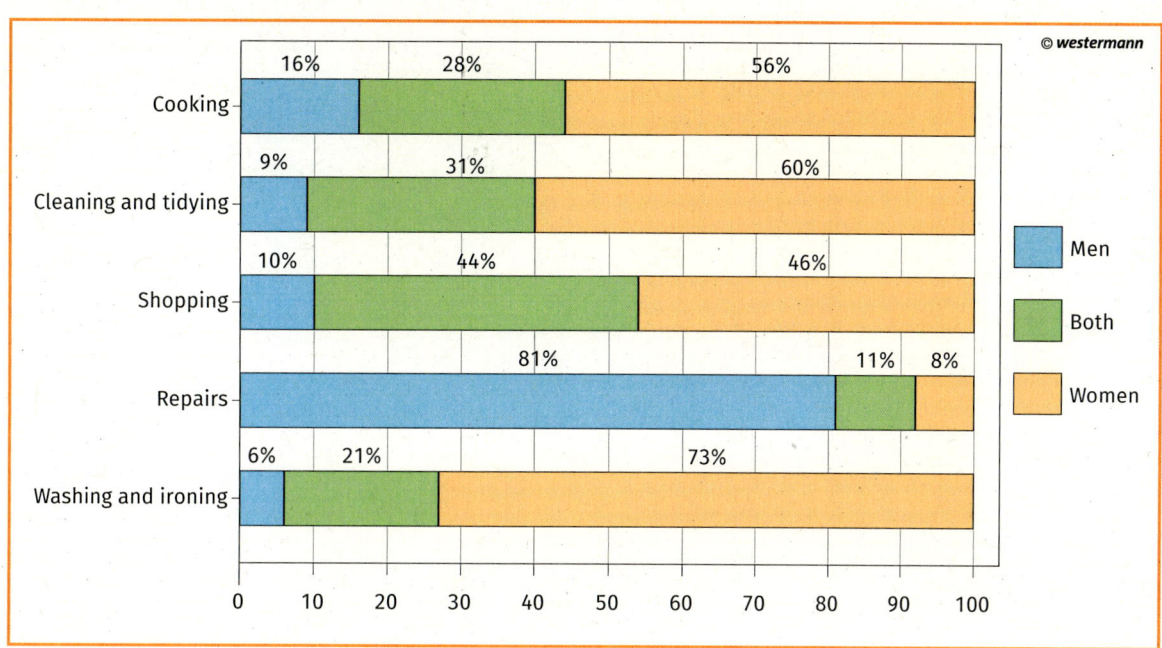

© westermann

1. _____% of men do the cooking.

2. 60% of women do the cleaning and _____.

3. 44% of both men and women do the _____.

4. _____% of men and _____% of women do the repairs.

5. _____% of women do the washing and ironing.

  b) **Check with your partner.**

  c) **Think about your family.**
   Who does what?
   Compare with your partner.

usually • normally • often •
never • always • sometimes • ...

In my family, my mother
normally does ...

My father never does ...

13 Your film poster

a) Make a poster for the film *Juno*.

16
p. 25

The film is about ... •
The main character is ... •
My favourite character is ... •
My favourite scene is ... •
I liked ... • I didn't like ... • ...

Denk darüber nach, was du auf deinem Poster haben willst, bevor du es erstellst. Du könntest z.B. alle Informationen zu deiner Lieblingsfigur suchen und Bilder ergänzen.
Du könntest dir auch einige der folgenden Fragen aussuchen und auf deinem Poster beantworten:

- Worum geht es im Film?
- Was passiert im Film?
- Wer ist die Hauptfigur?
- Welche Figuren gibt es noch im Film?
- Hat dir der Film gefallen? Warum / warum nicht?
- Was ist deine Lieblingsszene? Warum?

b) **Present your poster in class.**

Complete the wordbank.

Probleme, die Teenager haben können: (→ Seite 14, 15)

– *school problems*

_____

_____

Dinge, die du mit einer Person machst,   (→ Seite 15, 17, 18)
die du magst:

– *spend the afternoon together* _____

_____

_____

Wörter, die mit dem Film *Juno* zu tun haben: (→ Seite 20, 21)

– *teenage pregnancy* _____

_____

_____

Haushaltspflichten: (→ Seite 22, 23)

– *cooking* _____

_____

_____

Making it on your own

In diesem *Theme* ...

- liest du über Personen, die Englisch bei der Arbeit benötigen.
- sprichst du über deine Zukunftspläne.
- beschäftigst du dich mit dem Thema Kinderarbeit.
- erfährst du über Teenager, die versuchen, die Welt zu verbessern.

1 The start of something new

a) **Listen to the poem. What is it about? Tick.**

12

feelings at a school party ☐

feelings about leaving school ☐

b) **Listen again and read along.**

> School bell rings for one last time
> Oh how quickly seven years go by!
> The doors open, at last I'm free
> To be whoever I want to be.
> Goodbye teachers, goodbye rules
> Goodbye lessons, goodbye school.
>
> But now that the future is really here,
> All my hopes and dreams turn into fears,
> Will I find the right job and make new friends?
> So many questions
> And who knows how it will end!
>
> Am I ready to face the world alone?
> What if things don't go to plan?
> Am I ready to leave the safety of my home?
> What if the boy isn't ready to be a man …
>
> Zoe Carroll

c) **Underline what you do not understand.**
Talk about the text with a partner.

> Kannst du mir sagen,
> wie man „years go by"
> verstehen soll?

> Wenn man die ganze Zeile liest,
> kann man aus dem Zusammenhang
> verstehen, dass …

2 Job bingo

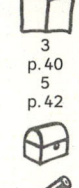

3
p. 40
5
p. 42

a) **Read the jobs. Mix them up and write them down.**

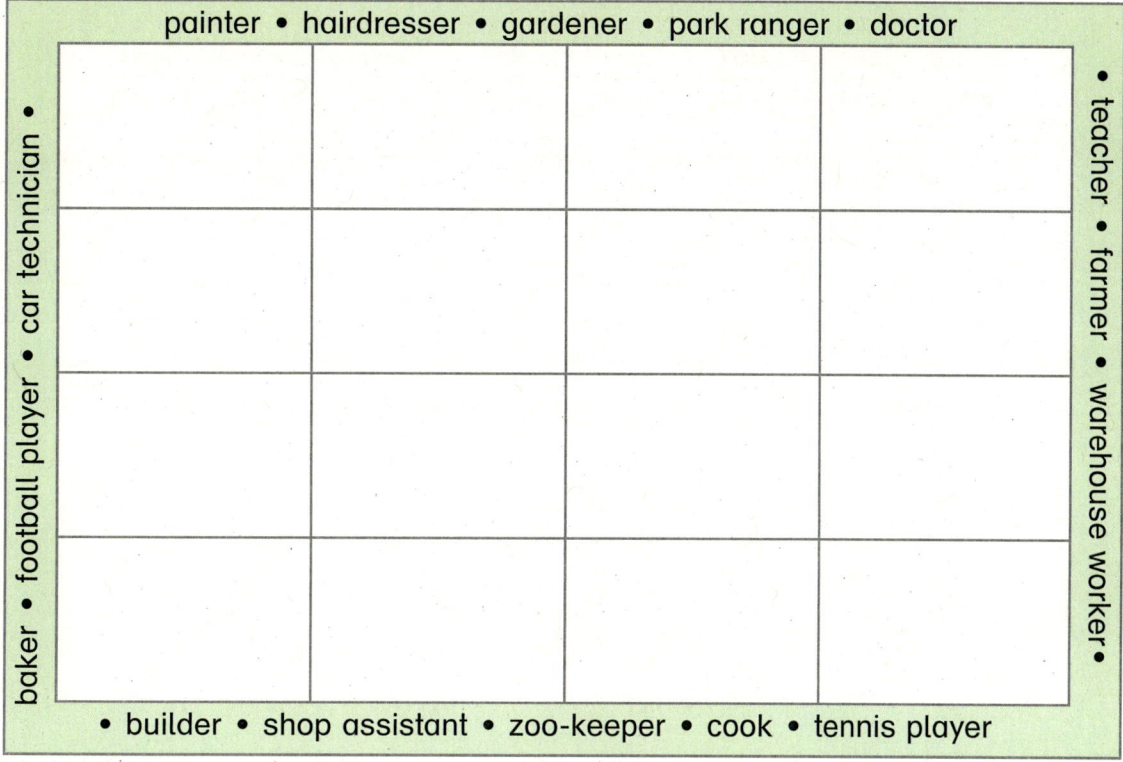

painter • hairdresser • gardener • park ranger • doctor

baker • football player • car technician •

• teacher • farmer • warehouse worker •

• builder • shop assistant • zoo-keeper • cook • tennis player

b) **Play bingo in class:**
    Listen to the job descriptions and circle the jobs.

13

> Um zu gewinnen, brauchst du vier eingekreiste Wörter
> – in einer Reihe,
> – in einer Spalte oder
> – diagonal.

c) **Play a new round of bingo**
    with your classmates.

> Die Materialien findest du
> bei Aufgabe II im Anhang.

He or she
works at a school.

A teacher.

3 Future plans

a) Listen to Ben. Circle his future plans in the word web.

1
p.40

14

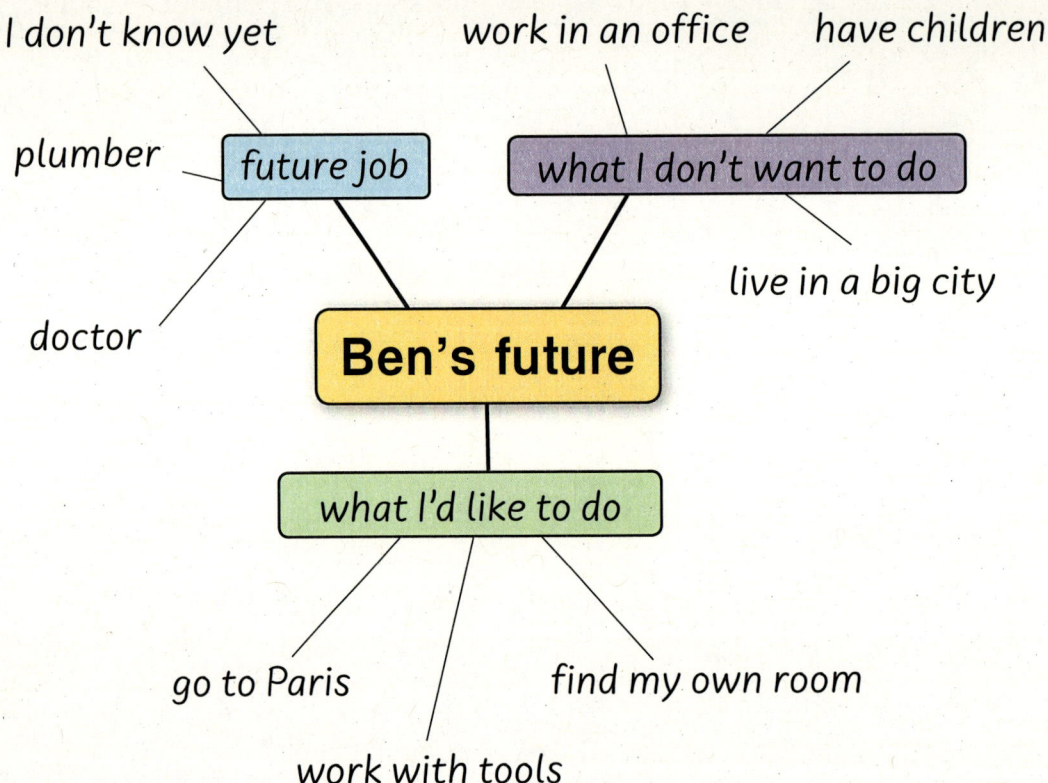

I don't know yet   work in an office   have children

plumber   future job   what I don't want to do

doctor

Ben's future

live in a big city

what I'd like to do

go to Paris   find my own room

work with tools

b) Look at a) again. Fill in the information for Ben.

name: _Ben_____

future job: _____

what he doesn't want to do: _____

_____

what he would like to do: _____

_____

_____

4 What's that job?

5/6
p. 42

a) Look at the pictures. Write down the jobs.

Zwei Jobs bleiben übrig.

waiter • baker • gardener • car technician • policeman • teacher

1

_____

2

_____

3

_____

4

_____

b) Read what the people say. Match the sentences and the jobs.

2 "I always wanted to teach English at a school."

"I like working with cars. I like getting my hands dirty."

"Many years ago, most of our bread was made in bakeries.

Today lots of bread is produced in factories."

"Sometimes I need to speak English, because tourists often

eat at the restaurant."

5 **Jessica**

Jessica left school two years ago.
She wrote a report for an international youth magazine.

a) **Listen and read along. Underline what Jessica does at the restaurant.**

7
p. 42

15

I learned English at school.
It was one of my favourite subjects.
After school I started an apprenticeship as a "Restaurantfachfrau".
Many people come to the restaurant for conferences and family parties. We decorate the rooms and the tables nicely and offer delicious meals and a good service.
I can practise my English whenever there are foreign guests in the restaurant.

Jessica (18)

b) **Cover the report with a sheet of paper.**
Then read the sentences. Are they true or false?

	true	false
1. One of Jessica's favourite subjects at school was English.	☐	☐
2. Many people come to the restaurant for breakfast and family parties.	☐	☐
3. She has to decorate the rooms and tables.	☐	☐
4. Jessica can practise her Spanish whenever there are foreign guests in the restaurant.	☐	☐

c) **Correct the false sentences from b).**

_____

_____

_____

_____

6 Torge

Torge also wrote a report for the international youth magazine.

a) Listen and read along.

7
p.42

16

I work as a joiner. I like my job very much. You can work in other countries if you join an organization called "Rolandsbrüder". They leave their home town and work in other companies to get more experience. I like this idea and have already spoken to colleagues for more information. Here I am in the special clothes of these craftsmen who travel around the world. I had some young joiners as guests from Ireland, France and Canada. My English was good enough to talk to them. We were taught to speak a lot at school and that helps me.

Torge (20)

b) Read again. Circle the correct words.

1. Torge works as a joiner / waiter.

2. You can work in other cities / countries if you join an

   organization called "Rolandsbrüder".

3. Torge has spoken to colleagues / friends for more information.

4. He spoke to his guests in German / English.

c) Read again. Complete the sentences.

1. To get more experience, the "Rolandsbrüder" leave _____

   _____

2. At school, Torge was taught _____

   _____

7 Your future plans

a) Make a word web with <u>your</u> future plans.

9
p.43

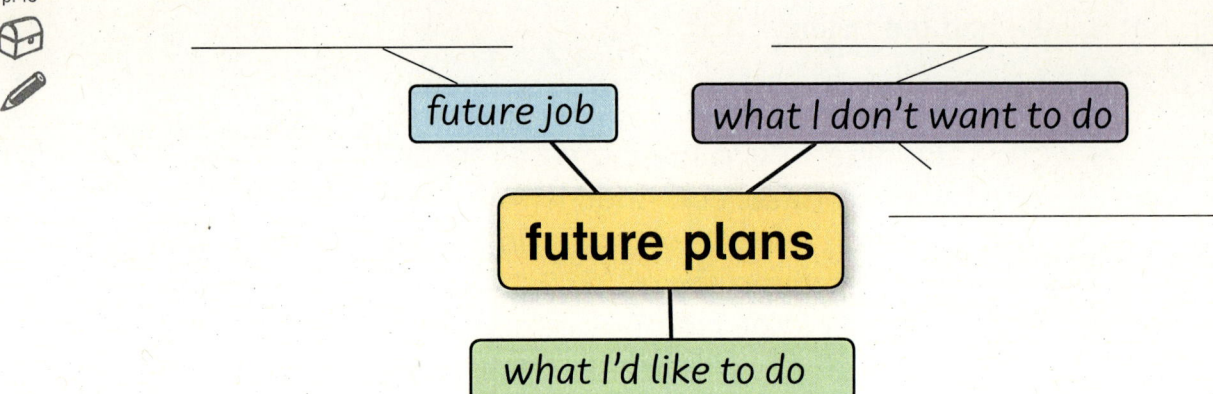

future job

what I don't want to do

future plans

what I'd like to do

b) Interview two classmates.
Complete the table.

What don't you want to do?

What's your future job?

What would you like to do?

	name: _____	name: _____
future job		
what he/she doesn't want to do		
what he/she would like to do		

c) Present your results in class.

I'd like to talk about Esther. She wants to be a baker.
She doesn't want to work in an office ...

8 **Child labour or chores?**

a) **Read the texts. Match the photos and the texts.**

Child labour:
A boy is making bricks
to build houses.
1

Chores:
A girl is emptying
the dishwasher.
2

Child labour:
Children are working
at a weaving machine.
3

Chores:
A boy is outside. He
is mowing the lawn.
4

Child labour:
A boy is making a
carpet.
5

Chores:
A girl is hoovering
at home.
6

b) **Complete the sentences.**

child labour • chore

1. A _____ is something you do at home to help in the

house. For example, emptying the dishwasher or hoovering.

2. _____ is when children work in very bad conditions.

c) **Talk to your partner. What chores do you do at home?**

9 Human rights

10 December is Human Rights Day. On this day human rights organisations talk to people about problems in the world.

p. 44/45

17

a) Listen to the dialogue and tick.

Ein Foto bleibt übrig.

  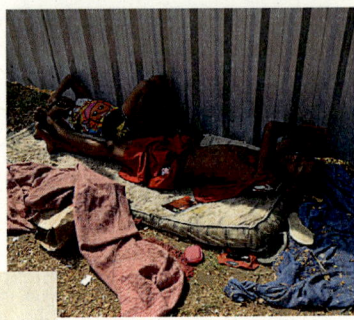

_____ _____ _____

_____ _____ _____

b) Label the photos in a).

child labour • homeless children • good education

c) Listen again. Is it true or false?

	true	false
1. Charlie is talking to a man from Amnesty International.		
2. He has got some information about child labour.		
3. Some children have to work 10 hours a day to support their families.		
4. A lot of children in the world have a good education.		
5. Amnesty International supports families in India and in Bangladesh.		

10 Charlie's article

Charlie wants to tell others about human rights organisations.
He wrote an article for the school magazine.

p.44/45

a) Form a group of four.
Each group member chooses one paragraph and reads it.

> Human rights organisations try to help these children.
> They write letters and emails.
> Sometimes they protest against problems in the world.
> Many organisations also collect money for
> poor children and families.

> Right now Amnesty International sells fair trade
> T-shirts to collect money for poor families in India
> and in Bangladesh. The money goes to the people
> who need it.

> Yesterday I met Jay Harris. He works for Amnesty
> International, a human rights organisation. He said
> that in some countries children can't go to school.
> They have to work to support their families.
> The children are often very young and have to work
> all day. They don't get a good education.

> **Human rights for everyone!**
> Human rights organisations help people all over
> the world. Many people need help because in their
> countries their rights are not respected.

b) Talk to your group members.
Tell them what your paragraph is about.

Ihr könnt euch auch auf
Deutsch unterhalten.

c) Put the paragraphs in the correct order (1-4).

d) Compare with your classmates.

11 Just a number?

11
p. 44

a) Look at the statistics.
Answer the questions in German.

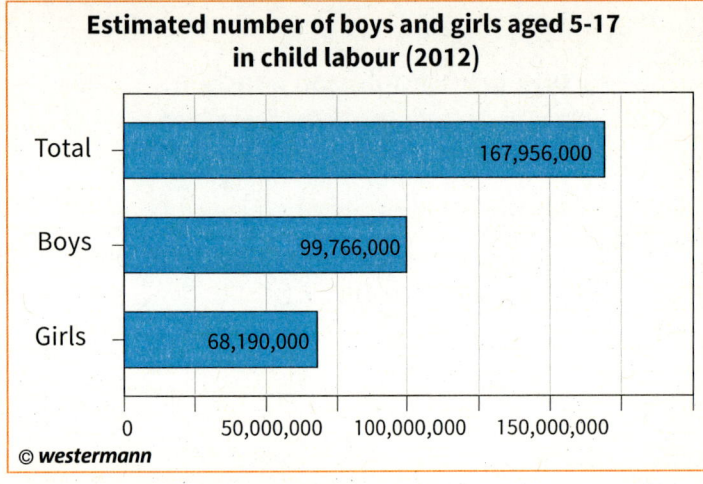

Estimated number of boys and girls aged 5-17 in child labour (2012)

Total — 167,956,000
Boys — 99,766,000
Girls — 68,190,000

0   50,000,000   100,000,000   150,000,000

© **westermann**

> Müssen mehr Jungen oder mehr Mädchen Kinderarbeit leisten?

> Wie viele Kinder sind von Kinderarbeit betroffen?

> Auf welches Alter bezieht sich die Untersuchung?

b) What else do you find out from the statistics?
Talk to your partner.

Land und Leute

Die Organisation der Vereinten Nationen, UN, wurde 1945 gegründet. Sie hat sich zum Ziel gesetzt, den Weltfrieden und die Einhaltung der Menschrechte zu sichern. 1989 veröffentlichte die UN das Übereinkommen über die Rechte des Kindes, in dem die Grundrechte der Kinder beschrieben werden: z.B. das Recht auf Bildung und Ausbildung und das Recht, mit der Familie in einem sicheren Zuhause zu leben. Die UN gründete 1946 die Organisation UNICEF, die sich speziell um die Rechte der Kinder kümmert. Heute unterstützt UNICEF etwa 150 Länder mit medizinischer und finanzieller Hilfe als auch mit Bildungsangeboten. Es gibt circa 150 Millionen Kinder, die arbeiten müssen, 37 Millionen Kinder, die auf der Flucht sind vor Krieg, Armut und Naturkatastrophen und eine große Anzahl von Kindern, die nicht zur Schule gehen können. Es gibt noch viel zu tun für UNICEF.

12 Changing the world for the better

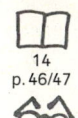 **14**
p. 46/47

 a) **Read Tariq's report. Tick.**

A soup kitchen is a place where …

you can learn to cook.

poor and homeless people get a hot meal.

Tariq, 16

My name is Tariq. I am 16 years old and I live in Philadelphia in the USA. I work as a volunteer in a soup kitchen twice a month. I got to know the soup kitchen when we did a project at high school about hunger and homeless people in our city. We visited the soup kitchen and talked to the people working there. When the project was finished, I thought about helping out myself. I contacted the woman who runs the soup kitchen. She was very happy to get my support. Now I help with cooking and serving meals. I also have to clean the kitchen and the tables. Homeless and poor people come to the soup kitchen for a hot meal. I really like my work here. It is great to see that they enjoy the food.

 b) **Read the questions. Write down short answers.**

1. Where does Tariq work? _____

2. How often does he work there? _____

3. How did he get to know the soup kitchen? _____

_____

4. What are his duties? _____

_____

5. Why does he like it? _____

_____

13 T-shirts

a) Read the statements on the T-shirts.

15
p. 47

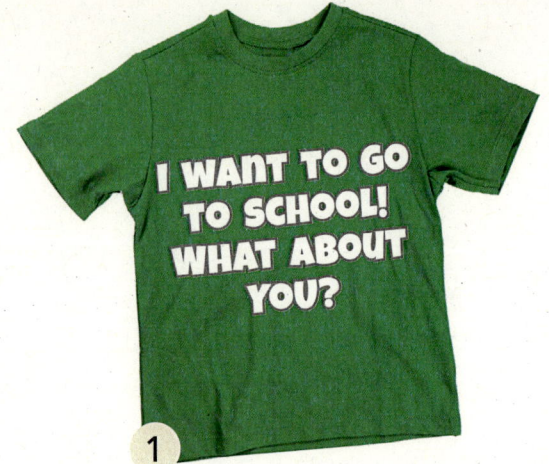

I WANT TO GO TO SCHOOL! WHAT ABOUT YOU?

1

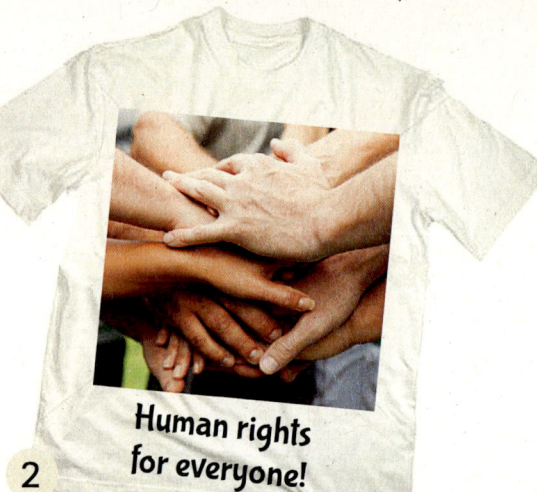

Human rights for everyone!

2

Stop child labour!

3

Support Amnesty International!

4

Schlage die Wörter im Wörterbuch nach.

b) Write down the German words.

human rights: _____

child labour: _____

support: _____

c) Explain the statements in German.

14 Your T-shirt

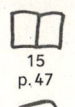

15
p. 47

a) Design <u>your</u> T-shirt with a statement.

Ideen findest du
bei Aufgabe 13.

 b) Present your T-shirt in class.

Complete the wordbank.

Berufe: (→ Seite 29, 31)

– *farmer* _____   _____

_____   _____

_____   _____

_____   _____

Dinge, die du in der Zukunft machen könntest: (→ Seite 30, 34)

– *find my own room* _____

_____

_____

Kinderarbeit: (→ Seite 35, 36)

– *some children work 10 hours a day* _____

_____

_____

Aussagen für Menschenrechte: (→ Seite 37, 40)

– *Stop child labour!* _____

_____

_____

3

South Africa –
The Rainbow Nation

In diesem *Theme* ...

• lernst du eine junge Deutsche kennen, die in Südafrika arbeitet.
• erfährst du einiges über die Sehenswürdigkeiten in Kapstadt.
• beschäftigst du dich mit Südafrikas Vergangenheit und Gegenwart.
• hältst du eine Präsentation über Südafrika.

1 Impressions of South Africa

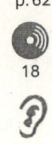

a) Look at Thabo's photos. Listen and point.

1
p. 62

18

b) Label the photos.

whale • drum • cable car • market • beach • safari

19

c) Listen and check.

I would love
to see / go …

d) Choose two photos.
Tell your partner what you would love to see or do.

2 Plans

3
p. 63

a) Read the messages.

Hi Isabel, I have a great idea – what about visiting my friend Baruti in Cape Town next weekend? 😎

Hey Thabo! That would be gr8! Could we stay 4 a whole week? There are some cheap flights!! 🙂

Yeah sure. 😊 We'll be out most of the time anyway. I'll call him now! Talk to you later 🙂

b) Read again. Circle the correct words.

1. Thabo's idea is to visit his friend in Cape Town / New York.

2. Isabel wants to stay there for a weekend / a week.

3. The flights are expensive / cheap.

4. Thabo will call Baruti now / later.

3 A boarding pass

4
p. 63

a) Read Isabel's boarding pass.

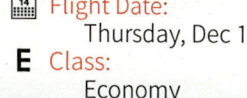
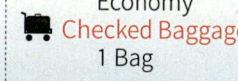

BOARDING PASS

You have successfully checked in for your flight(s). See details below:

Important Information:
All flights are non-smoking. Smoking is forbidden at all times during the flight.

Passenger:
Ms Isabel Weber
From:
Nelspruit, Mpumalanga
To:
Cape Town
Seat:
17B
Boarding Time:
21:35

Flight:
TAPO336
Booking Reference:
DM0345
Flight Date:
Thursday, Dec 14
E Class:
Economy
Checked Baggage:
1 Bag

b) Work with a partner. Ask and answer questions in German.

Wohin fliegt Isabel?

Sie fliegt nach Kapstadt. Wann ...?

4 Sightseeing in Cape Town

5-6
p. 64-65

20

a) Listen and read along.

Cape Town is the second largest city in South Africa. It has 3.7 million inhabitants. Cape Town is great for shopping. It offers lots of different things, from jewellery and traditional African art to designer labels and diamonds. Visit one of the shopping malls or flea markets for presents and souvenirs.

Table Mountain offers amazing views of the city and the ocean.
You can take a cable car to the top of the mountain.
Don't forget to take a jacket because it can often be cool on the mountain top.

Two Oceans Aquarium is located on the V&A Waterfront.
You can see many different animals that live in the sea. There are over 3,000 sea animals, including sharks, fish, turtles and penguins.

Robben Island was the prison where Nelson Mandela and many other famous black freedom fighters were held. You can have a tour of the island and the prison. A tour takes three and a half hours.

b) **Read again. Is it true or false?**

	true	false
1. Cape Town is the second largest city in Australia.	☐	☐
2. You can buy jewellery, diamonds and more in Cape Town.	☐	☐
3. You don't need a jacket because it can often be hot on Table Mountain.	☐	☐
4. You can see sharks and lions at Two Oceans Aquarium.	☐	☐
5. A tour of Robben Island and the prison takes three and a half hours.	☐	☐

c) **Correct the false sentences from b).**

_____

_____

_____

_____

_____

d) **Choose one thing you would do in Cape Town. Talk to your partner about it. Say why.**

> I **would** take a cable car to the top of Table Mountain, **because** the view looks amazing! **What would you do?**

> I **would** visit ...

5 Isabel's tour

7/9
p.65

21

a) Listen and number.

Zwei Aussagen bleiben übrig.

"We went to Robben Island."

"We visited Two Oceans Aquarium."

"We saw the Empire State Building."

1 "We went up Table Mountain."

"We did some shopping at a flea market."

"We met Baruti in front of the flea market."

"We visited the Castle of Good Hope."

"We saw the Clock Tower at the Waterfront."

b) Write a list of the places Isabel saw in the right order.

1. Table Mountain _____   _____

2. _____   _____

_____   _____

 c) Check with your partner.

 d) Put the pictures from Isabel's tour in the correct order. Glue them onto the next page.

Die Bilder findest du bei Aufgabe III im Anhang.

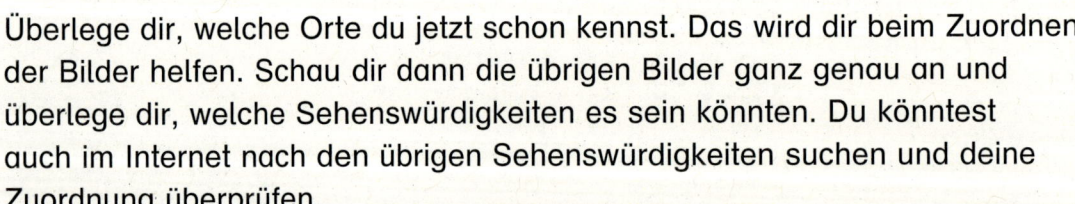

Überlege dir, welche Orte du jetzt schon kennst. Das wird dir beim Zuordnen der Bilder helfen. Schau dir dann die übrigen Bilder ganz genau an und überlege dir, welche Sehenswürdigkeiten es sein könnten. Du könntest auch im Internet nach den übrigen Sehenswürdigkeiten suchen und deine Zuordnung überprüfen.

Bevor du die Bilder auf die Seite klebst, vergleiche deine Reihenfolge mit der deines Partners oder deiner Partnerin, um zu prüfen, ob deine richtig ist.

Isabel's tour of Cape Town

1

2

3

4

5

6

 e) Talk to a partner about Isabel's tour.
What did she see or do at the places?

First, Isabel went ...
Then, she ...

 f) Which tour would you take?
Present your tour in class.

8 Photos from South Africa

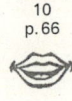

10
p. 66

a) Look at the photos. Match them to the texts.

A woman is washing her clothes in front of her hut in the slums of Johannesburg. South Africa still has two faces.

Between 1948 and 1991 the sign "EUROPEANS BLANKES" showed that the bench was only for white people. The black man is not allowed to sit on it.

Nelson Mandela is holding a speech against apartheid.

Today, black and white children have equal rights and play together on the beaches.

 b) Check with a partner.

9 Nelson Mandela

12
p. 67

22

a) Listen and read along.

Nelson Mandela was the first democratically elected president of South Africa (1994-1999). He spent most of his life fighting against apartheid. Apartheid was a political system in which non-whites were separated and discriminated against.
Mandela was a leading member of the African National Congress (ANC).
The ANC fights for black rights. It has been the ruling party in South Africa since 1994.

In 1964, Mandela was sentenced to life imprisonment because of his work for the ANC. He spent 26 years in prison.
In 1993 he won the Nobel Peace Prize with Frederik de Klerk, the president who ended apartheid.
Mandela believed in a society where whites and non-whites could live together peacefully.
He died in 2013 at the age of 95.

b) Read the questions. Underline the answers in the text:

1. When was Nelson Mandela president of South Africa? un
2. What was apartheid? un
3. What happened to Mandela in 1964? un
4. When did he win the Nobel Peace Prize? un

c) Write down the answers from b).

1. _____

2. _____

3. _____

4. _____

d) Compare with your partner.

 **Land und Leute**

Kapstadt wurde 1652 von Jan van Riebeeck, einem niederländischen Kaufmann, als Zwischenstopp für holländische Schiffe auf dem Weg nach Indien gegründet. Als mehr und mehr holländische Siedler kamen, nahmen diese sich das Land der Eingeborenen, um eine eigene Farm und eine holländische Siedlung aufzubauen. Während des 19. Jahrhunderts entwickelten die weißen Siedler eine eigene Nationalität. Sie nannten sich „Boers" oder „Afrikaner".

1948 führten sie das Apartheid System ein, das schwarze und weiße Menschen voneinander trennte. Schließlich unternahm die Regierung 1990 die ersten Schritte gegen die Diskriminierung von Schwarz und Weiß.

Als Nelson Mandela 1994 freigelassen wurde, wurde er der 1. Präsident des Landes, der durch demokratische Wahlen an die Regierung kam. Heute setzt sich Südafrika für die Rassengleichheit ein, aber immer noch fühlen sich viele Schwarze nicht gleichberechtigt. Es bleibt noch viel zu tun.

10 Gimme hope Jo'anna

13
p. 68

a) Listen to Eddie Grant's anti-apartheid song from 1988. What does "Jo'anna" stand for? Tick.

23

☐ Eddie's girlfriend ☐ Johannesburg

b) Read the chorus.

> Du könntest auch den ganzen Text im Internet suchen.

[...]
Gimme hope Jo'anna, Hope Jo'anna
Gimme hope Jo'anna
'Fore the morning come
Gimme hope Jo'anna, Hope Jo'anna
Hope before the morning come
[...]

c) Tell a partner in German what the chorus means.

> Ich glaube, „gimme" bedeutet ..

> Meiner Meinung nach soll das Lied ...

11 What apartheid meant

14
p.69

a) **Read about Moloko, a boy from South Africa.**

My dad and my granddad had to do jobs that white people didn't want to do.
They didn't really have a choice and they got paid really badly. They weren't allowed to vote or travel.
That's different now, I can go to school and I have a job that I like.
But black and white people still live separate lives most of the time.
White people go to sports clubs that other white people go to and so on.

b) **Read the text again. Find out about:**

what life was like in the past  un

what life is like now in the present un

c) **Read about Phumzile, a girl from South Africa.**
Underline the information from b).

25 years ago black people weren't allowed to buy bread in the same shops as whites.
We couldn't go to the same schools as they did.
That's all different now, now we're the Rainbow Nation.
People from many different backgrounds can live together peacefully.
But racism still exists at work and everywhere else. I hope that will change one day.

d) **Compare with your partner.**
Talk about the information
in German.

In der Vergangenheit mussten der Vater und Opa von Moloko ...

12   About South Africa

15
p. 69

Make a presentation about South Africa:

1. Choose <u>one</u> of the topics:
   - sightseeing in South Africa
   - history of South Africa

2. Collect information about your topic.
   You can use information
   from this chapter or search for
   more information on the Internet.

3. Take notes. You can look up words in a dictionary.

4. Collect photos and pictures
   for a poster. You can draw
   them or use pictures from the Internet.

5. Design your poster.

6. Do your presentation in class.

My topic: _____

_____

_____

_____

_____

_____

_____

_____

_____

_____

_____

_____

_____

_____

_____

Complete the wordbank.

Wörter und Dinge, die du mit Südafrika verbindest: (→ Seite 44, 46)

— *safari*

_____   _____

_____   _____

_____   _____

Sehenswürdigkeiten in Kapstadt: (→ Seite 46, 47)

— *Table Mountain*

_____

_____

Wörter und Phrasen, die du mit (→ Seite 51)
Nelson Mandela verbindest:

— *against apartheid*

_____

_____

Südafrikas Vergangenheit: (→ Seite 50, 53)

— *black people weren't allowed to vote*

_____

_____

Südafrikas Gegenwart: (→ Seite 50, 53)

— *Rainbow Nation*

_____

Changes and challenges

4

In diesem *Theme* ...

- beschäftigst du dich mit dem Thema Naturkatastrophen.
- erfährst du etwas über die Auswirkungen von Tornados und wie man sich davor schützen kann.
- sprichst du darüber, was man im Internet machen kann.
- liest du darüber, wie man online sicher gehen kann.
- diskutierst du, welche Informationen du im Internet veröffentlichen würdest.

1 Natural disasters

a) Look at the pictures and listen.

1

drought

2

3

5

4

 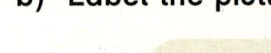
b) Label the pictures.

tornado • drought • earthquake • flood • wildfire

 c) Match the pictures and the texts.

Zwei Bilder bleiben übrig.

This is when the ground is dry from the hot sun.

This is what can happen if it rains too much.

This is dangerous rotating air. It usually starts on the land.

 d) Check with your partner.

2 A problem in Oklahoma

a) Read the article. What is it about?

  It is about …

   an earthquake   a tornado   in Oklahoma.

**DEADLY TWISTER
DESTROYS TOWN**

A killer twister hit Oklahoma yesterday.
At least 8 people are dead and many
more are injured. The violent tornado
destroyed large areas of the state.
The small town of Lone Grove was
one of the worst hit by the tornado.
Luke Denton (42) has lived in Lone Grove all his life.
He said, "It blew right through the middle of town – I've never seen
anything like it. It was a monster. I was so scared!"
Mrs Denton (39) told us, "We're just lucky to be alive."
The couple's house was lifted off the ground and completely destroyed
by the storm.
Now the storm is moving east. There are fears that the Mid-South, which
was destroyed by last month's storms, will be hit again.

  b) Read again. Match the sentence parts.

1 A killer twister	were destroyed.
2 Large areas of Oklahoma	is moving east.
3 Lone Grove	was completely destroyed.
4 Luke Denton	*1* hit Oklahoma yesterday.
5 The couple's house	was so scared.
6 Now the storm	was one of the worst hit.

3 A crossword

Auf Seite 58 findest du Hilfe.

p.82/83

a) Write down the words for the photos.

A

B

C

D

E

A

B | | | 7 | | 8 | | | 9 |

10

C | | | 2 | | | 5 | |

4

D | | 3 | | | | | | | | 6 |

E | | | 1 | |

b) Write down the new natural disaster.

v _ _ c _ _ _ c _ _ _ p _ i _ n
1 2   3 4 5   6 7 8   9   10

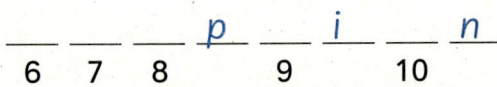

Du kannst ein Wörterbuch benutzen.

c) Write down the German word for the natural disaster in b).

_____

4 **A survival story**

a) **Listen. What is the boy talking about?**

The boy is talking about ...

☐ a tornado   ☐ a flood   in his town.

5
p.84

25

b) **Listen again.**
Complete the sentences.

> Du kannst dir die Geschichte mehrmals anhören.

> loud • ~~alive~~ • happy • trees • destroyed •
> basement • sad • tornado • scared

1. "My name is Alex. I'm 15 years old and I live in Lone Grove.

   I'm lucky to be _alive_____."

2. "We were warned about the _____ on TV

   just before it happened."

3. "I was really _____."

4. "We all ran to the _____."

5. "We waited for hours. The storm was really _____."

6. "When we came out, everything was _____."

7. "The tornado had lifted our house off the ground and pulled all

   the _____ out of the ground."

8. "There was nothing left. We are all so _____."

9. "But I am _____ that my family and I are still alive.

c) **Check with your partner.**

d) **Read out the story in class.**

5 A tornado warning

a) Match the pictures and the sentences.

 **1**   Always stay away from windows.

 **2**   If you are outside,
take shelter in a building.

 **3**   If you have a pet, take it with you.

 **4**   Get under a strong piece of
furniture, for example a table.

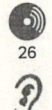

b) Listen and check.

c) Talk to a partner.
Explain the sentences in a) in German.

> Bei einem Tornado soll
> man immer ...

> Genau, und wenn man ...

d) Listen to the full warning.
Write down two more tips. Draw pictures for them.

_____

_____

_____

_____

6 Warning systems

7
p. 85

28

a) Listen and read along.

It is difficult to know when there will be tornadoes.
But meteorologists can tell when they might form.
They send up weather balloons every twelve hours.
The balloons carry equipment.
This equipment measures things like the temperature.
With these measurements, meteorologists can tell when a tornado might form.

Meteorologists can also use a modern kind of weather radar.
They can detect a tornado up to 20 minutes before it touches down.
Then they have time to release tornado warnings.

b) Find the English words in the article.
   Write down the German words.

> Benutze ein Wörterbuch.

1. meteorologist   – _____

2. form   – _____

3. equipment   – _____

4. measurements   – _____

5. detect   – _____

6. release warnings – _____

c) Check with your partner.

7 **Keeping in touch**

People have always looked for ways to keep in touch with their family and friends.

10
p.86

a) **Look at the pictures. Which inventions do you know?**

P

L

A

D

U

O

 b) **Match the pictures and the sentences.**

2000 years ago, pigeons were used to send information about the Olympic Games in Athens.

The telephone was invented in 1876.

The first computers were sold in the USA in 1950.

The first email was sent in 1965.

The first call on a mobile phone was made in 1973.

In 2002 many people started using social networks.

c) **Complete the sentence with the letters from b).**

On the Internet you can ____ ____ ____ ____ ____ ____ photos.

8 On the Internet

a) **Look at the pictures.**
   Say what you can and can't do on the Internet.

> You can't try on shoes on the Internet.

b) **Complete the sentences.**
   What can you do on the Internet? What can't you do?

> search for • chat • go dancing • watch • drink • talk to •
> go swimming • download • upload • try on • buy • …

– On the Internet you *can …*_____ information.

– You _____ photos.

– People _____ clothes.

– You _____ with your friends.

– I _____ shoes.

– I _____.

– _____.

– _____.

c) **Compare with your partner.**

9 On the phone

a) Listen to the telephone call. What is it about?

11
p.87

29

It is about problems with ...

friends. teachers. parents.

b) Listen again. Then match the sentence parts.

1 Justin had an argument   online every evening.

2 They don't want him to spend   when homework is boring.

3 His parents think   too much time online.

4 Tessa watches videos   with his parents.

5 Tessa spends three hours   Justin is wasting his time.

c) Talk to your classmates. Then complete the table.

How long are you
online every day?

About 30 minutes
every day.

About 2 hours
every day.

name	How long?

d) Collect your results in class.

10 Online communication

12
p.87

a) **Read the texts.**
Then underline pros **and cons** un ✏ **for smartphones.**

I can't live without my smartphone! I never get bored because I can always do something with it – it is a phone, a camera, a radio and an MP3 player all in one. With my smartphone I can keep in touch with my friends. It is also great that I won't get lost. I can always check the way on my smartphone. But sometimes I think I should go out more often and meet my friends for a chat in town.

Dara, 17

I sold my smartphone two weeks ago. I was so distracted by all the apps. Sometimes I had hundreds of messages on my phone. I was really stressed out because I thought I had to read and answer all of them. The moment when I decided to sell my phone was when I had a date with a girl I had met online. We were in a café and checked our phones every two minutes. We didn't really talk to each other. That was annoying.

Lawrence, 18

b) **Read again. Then complete the table.**

pros	cons
– you never get bored	– you are distracted by apps

c) **Talk to your classmates.**

I think it's silly to be online all the time ...

In my opinion, smartphones are very helpful.

...

11   Talking on the radio

p. 88/89

30

a)   Listen to the radio show.
Circle the correct names.

Ein Name bleibt übrig.

Lee   Brian   Kelly   Anna

b)   Tick their Internet experiences.

☐   a friend is always online   ☐   a computer virus

☐   a broken DVD   ☐   cyberbullying

c)   Listen again. Who had the experiences?
Fill in the names.

Du kannst diese Aufgabe auch in einer
Kleingruppe bearbeiten und dich auf eine Person
konzentrieren. Später tauscht ihr euch aus.

1. _____'s friend is always online.

2. _____ got a DVD too late to give it as a
birthday present.

3. _____ bought a broken DVD online.

4. _____ put some photos of himself on the Internet.

5. _____ got mean comments from some bullies.

d)   Talk to your classmates. Look at c) for help.
Has something like that ever happened to <u>you</u> or to one of your friends?

Yes, my friend ...

No, I've never had
any problems.

Yes, I also ...

12 How to stay safe online

There are lots of organisations that try to make the Internet safe.
This is a flyer from one of them.

14
p.88

a) **Read the flyer. What is the most important tip for you? Why?**

S SAFE: Don't give out personal information
(full name, email, home address, school name)
to people who you don't trust.

M MEETING: It can be dangerous to meet someone
you only know online. Tell your parents about it or
ask someone you trust to come with you.

A ACCEPTING: Never accept emails or messages
and don't open files from people you don't know.
It can lead to serious problems because of viruses.

R RELIABLE: Sometimes people online lie about
who they are. They often put wrong information
on the Internet like a wrong name and age.

T TELL: If something or someone makes you feel
uncomfortable or if you are being bullied online,
tell your parents, friends or teachers.

b) **Answer the questions in German.**

1. Was sollte man zur Sicherheit nicht ins Internet stellen?
2. Was ist zu beachten, wenn man jemanden aus dem Internet treffen möchte?
3. Warum kann man einigen E-Mails oder Dateien nicht trauen?
4. Warum kann man nicht alles glauben, was Menschen über sich im Internet schreiben?
5. Wen kann man um Hilfe bitten, wenn man sich im Internet bedroht fühlt?

 **Land und Leute**

Mehr als 3,6 Milliarden Menschen weltweit nutzen heute das Internet. Das Internet wurde erfunden, weil die US Air Force ein sicheres System brauchte, mit dem sie Informationen verschicken konnte.

Die erste Version des Internets nannte man 'Arpanet': 1970 wurden zum ersten Mal Computer aus verschiedenen Ländern miteinander verbunden. Das Internet wurde nur von Wissenschaftlern benutzt. Dies änderte sich in den neunziger Jahren, als das World Wide Web (WWW) entwickelt wurde. Man nutzte das Internet von zu Hause. Heute gibt es nicht viel, was man nicht mit dem Internet machen kann. Man kann Informationen zu jedem Thema finden, Kleidung bestellen, Musik herunterladen, mit Freunden chatten, etc. Die Liste ist lang.

13 A computer cartoon

p. 88-89

a) **Match the cartoon to one of the sentences.**

1 "Let's download some videos."

2 "I wouldn't get too close. I have a really bad virus."

3 "Would you like to listen to some music?"

 b) **Compare with your partner.**

14 A social network profile

a) **Read Tessa's profile. What can you find out about her?**

14
p. 88

> Tessa is ...

> She was born ...

> Tessa is interested in ...

News (230) ▼   Favourites ▼

Tessa Barinski

Gender:	female
Birthday:	24 July 2000
Home town:	Bristol, UK
Relationship status:	single
Email:	T_B_2000@goggle.co.uk
Looking for:	friendship, dating
Political views:	not interested in politics, soooo boring!

Friends (127)

More friends (▼)

Personal information

Hobbies:	watching TV, parties, playing football, meeting friends, drinking, having fun, reading
Interests:	cinema, being online
Favourite music:	Hip Hop, R & B
Favourite TV shows:	The Vampire Diaries, Mad Men
Favourite films:	Twilight
Favourite books:	Twelve, Slam
About me:	I love parties!!!

---

b) **Make your own profile. Which information would only your friends see?**

> Eine Vorlage findest du bei Aufgabe IV im Anhang.

Only my friends would see ...

_____

_____

_____

 c) **Compare with your partner.**

Complete the wordbank.

Naturkatastrophen: (→ Seite 58, 60)

– *drought*
_____   _____

_____   _____

Dinge, die man im Internet machen kann: (→ Seite 65)

– *search for information*
_____

_____

_____

Pro- und Kontro-Argumente für den Gebrauch   (→ Seite 67)
von Smartphones:

– *you are distracted by apps*
_____

_____

_____

Informationen, die auf einem Profil in einem   (→ Seite 50, 53)
sozialen Netzwerk stehen können:

– *gender*
_____   _____

_____   _____

_____   _____

Theme 5

Exam practice

In diesem *Theme* ...

- kannst du verschiedene Übungsformen üben.
- kannst du die Fertigkeiten üben: Hören, Lesen, Schreiben, Mediation und Sprechen.
- findest du Hinweise und Erklärungen der unterschiedlichen Übungsformen.

Listening

Diese Tipps helfen dir beim Lösen von Höraufgaben:

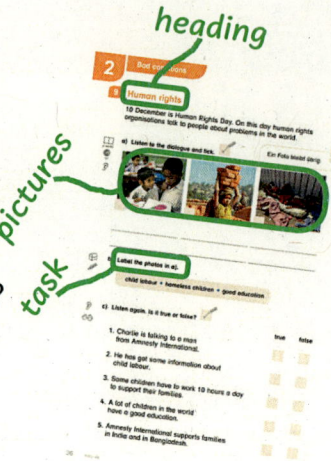

Vor dem Hören

Bevor du einen Text hörst, achte auf Folgendes:
- Wie lautet die **Überschrift** der Aufgabe?
  Gibt sie Hinweise, worum es im Hörtext gehen könnte?
- Gibt es **Bilder** zur Aufgabe? Was ist zu sehen?
- Überlege vor dem Hören, worum es gehen könnte.
  Weißt du schon etwas über das Thema?
  Was erwartest du?

Nun lies dir die **Aufgabenstellung** genau durch.
Manchmal sollst du nur heraushören, worum es **allgemein** geht.
Dann musst du nur grob verstehen, worum es geht.
Manchmal musst du aber auch **Einzelheiten** heraushören.
Dann ist es gut, wenn du besonders konzentriert zuhörst.

Während des Hörens

Höre dir das Gespräch oder die Geschichte einmal ganz an.
Versuche herauszufinden, worum es geht.
Achte dabei auf bekannte Wörter. Sie können dir helfen,
den Inhalt zu verstehen.

Die **Hintergrundgeräusche und die Stimmen** verraten oft schon viel, z. B.:
- Wo findet das Gespräch statt? (am Bahnhof, in der Schule, auf der Straße …)
- Wie fühlen sich die Sprecher? (begeistert, aufgeregt, traurig …)

Lies dir die Aufgabe erneut durch. Höre dir dann den Hörtext **ein zweites Mal** an.

Du kannst auch die folgende Tabelle benutzen.
Die **Fragen** helfen dir beim Verstehen eines Hörtextes:

Who?	Where?	When?	What?	How?	Why?
Wer spricht? Um wen geht es?	**Wo** findet das Gespräch/ die Geschichte statt?	**Wann** findet das Gespräch/ die Geschichte statt?	**Was** passiert? Worüber wird gesprochen?	**Wie** wird gesprochen? Wie fühlen sich die Sprecher?	**Warum** findet das Gespräch statt?

Multiple choice

Bei diesen Aufgaben ist von den angebotenen drei Antworten immer
nur <u>eine</u> Antwort richtig. Höre genau zu und lass dich nicht täuschen!
In den falschen Antworten können nämlich Wörter enthalten sein,
die auf den ersten Blick richtig erscheinen.
Die Aufgaben sind immer in der Reihenfolge des Hörtextes.
So kannst du dich besser orientieren.

1 **Leonie**

Leonie has just finished school.
Now she wants to visit Great Britain.

Listen to Leonie. Circle the correct answers.

1. Leonie is …

   15 / 16 / 17   years old.

2. She will go to …

   Wales / Scotland / England.

3. She will go by …

   car / plane / ship.

4. She will arrive at …

   London Heathrow Airport / Holborn Station / London Stansted Airport.

5. She will go to the city centre by …

   bus / train / car.

6. She will stay for …

   2 days / 7 days / 2 weeks.

7. She will stay at …

   a hotel / her friend's flat / a youth hostel.

Table completion

Bei diesen Aufgaben sollst du eine Tabelle mit den richtigen Informationen ergänzen. Die Personen im Hörtext sprechen nacheinander.
Bearbeite zuerst die erste Zeile und anschließend die zweite Zeile.

2 **Train to London**

Leonie meets two teenagers on her way to London.

32–33

Listen to the dialogues.
Then complete the table.

	Where from?	Age?	On the way to?	Wants to visit?
Rashid				
Charlotte	Australia			

Matching

Bei diesen Aufgaben erhältst du verschiedene Informationen, die du richtig zuordnen sollst. Das können Satzanfänge und Satzenden sein oder Namen und Bilder. Pass gut auf: Oft bleibt eine Möglichkeit übrig, z. B. ein Bild, ein Name, ein Satzende …

3 **A family photo**

Leonie meets Ron at the youth hostel. He shows her a photo of his family.

34

Listen. Match the names and the people.
There is <u>one more</u> name than you need.

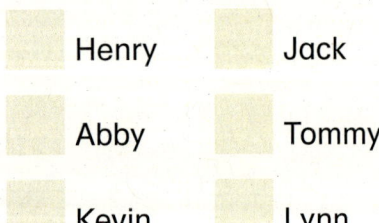

Henry   Jack

Abby   Tommy

Kevin   Lynn

Roberta

Reading

Diese Tipps helfen dir beim Lösen von Leseaufgaben:

Vor dem Lesen
Bevor du einen Text liest, achte auf Folgendes:
- Wie lautet die **Überschrift** des Textes?
  Gibt sie Hinweise, worum es gehen könnte?
- Gibt es **Bilder** zum Text? Was ist zu sehen?
- **Oft weißt du schon etwas über das Thema.**
  Das kann dir beim Verstehen des Textes helfen.

Während des Lesens
Überfliege den Text zuerst. Dabei musst du nicht jedes Wort verstehen.
Beim Überfliegen kannst du die wichtigsten Wörter (**keywords**) unterstreichen.
Manchmal reichen diese Wörter schon aus, um zu verstehen, worum es im Text geht.

Wenn du einen längeren Text liest, hilft es oft, wenn du ihn in **kleinere Abschnitte**
unterteilst. Versuche, für jeden Abschnitt eine Überschrift zu finden.
Dann verstehst du schon viel mehr.

Schau dir noch einmal die **Aufgabenstellung** an.
Hast du sie genau verstanden? Weißt du, worauf du achten sollst?

Was machst du, wenn du Wörter nicht direkt verstehst?
- Du kannst versuchen, **unbekannte Wörter** aus dem **Textzusammenhang** zu
  verstehen. Manchmal darfst du in deiner Prüfung auch ein **Wörterbuch** benutzen.
  Dann kannst du unbekannte Wörter nachschlagen. Schlage aber nur die Wörter
  nach, die du unbedingt zum Verstehen des Textes brauchst.
- Oft hilft es, dass viele Wörter im Englischen und im Deutschen
  ähnlich oder sogar gleich sind, z. B. *team – Team, long – lang, hair – Haar.*

Lies den Text noch einmal **gründlich** durch.
Beim Suchen nach genauen Informationen
kannst du **Fragen an den Text** stellen,
z. B. mit *who, where, when, what, how, why.*

Sentence halves

Bei diesen Aufgaben sollst du Satzhälften miteinander verbinden.
Lies dir zuerst den Text durch. Schau dir dann die angebotenen
Satzhälften genau an. Je zwei passen zusammen.

4 **London sights**

a) **Read the page from a city guide.**

Portobello Market in Notting Hill is the largest market in London. Here you can buy clothes, antiques and many other things. You can also try delicious food and listen to live music.

The Queen lives in Buckingham Palace when she is in London. You can watch the Changing of the Guard several times a day or even visit the palace.

Enjoy the view from the London Eye. On a nice day you have a great view: you can see three airports, 13 football stadiums and 36 bridges.

b) **Match the correct sentence parts. Complete the table.**

1	Portobello Market is …
2	At this market you can …
3	Several times a day you can …
4	From the London Eye you can …

A	watch the guards at the palace.
B	enjoy a great view.
C	buy many different things.
D	the largest market in London.

1	2	3	4

Short answers

Bei diesen Aufgaben sollst du Fragen zum Text kurz beantworten.
Du sollst <u>keine</u> ganzen Sätze schreiben.

5 Diwali

 a) Read the information.

In India 84% of the people are Hindus.
One of their festivals is Diwali.
It is in October or November.
Diwali is the festival of lights.
It lasts five days. At Diwali people wear
new clothes and light candles inside
and outside their homes. Families and
friends meet. They give each other presents.
They usually have a great meal. There are fireworks and lots of
families go to the temple. Diwali is also the start of the new year for
Hindus all over the world.

 b) Read the questions. Then write down short answers.

1. How many people in India are Hindus?

_____

2. Which festival do Hindus celebrate in October or November?

_____

3. What is Diwali?

_____

4. What happens at Diwali?

_____

5. When does the new year start for Hindus?

_____

Writing

Diese Tipps helfen dir beim Schreiben von Texten:

Vor dem Schreiben
Lies dir die **Aufgabenstellung** genau durch und überlege:

- Was für eine **Art von Text** sollst du schreiben? (E-Mail, Bericht für die Schülerzeitung, Geschichte ...)
- **An wen** richtet sich der Text? (an einen Freund, eine Gastfamilie, einen Firmenchef ...)
- **Was solltest du schreiben**? (welche Inhalte, richtige Anrede und Grußformel bei Briefen, Beantworten von Fragen ...)
- **Wie viel Zeit** hast du, um deinen Text zu schreiben?

Plane deinen Text:
- Lege dir ein **Wortnetz oder eine Liste** an. Dabei merkst du meist schon, welche Wörter du noch nachschlagen musst.
- Vergleiche deine Ideen noch einmal mit der Aufgabenstellung. Hast du **alle Punkte der Aufgabenstellung** bedacht?
- Sammle **Satzanfänge und Ausdrücke**, die für deinen Text wichtig sind. Sollst du z. B. einen Brief schreiben, solltest du unbedingt an die Anrede und die Grußformel am Ende denken. Denke auch an ähnliche Texte, die du schon einmal gesehen hast. Oft findest du darin Sätze, die du benutzen kannst.
- Mache dir ein paar **Notizen mit möglichen Formulierungen**. Schreibst du einen Brief an einen Freund, kannst du z. B. etwas lockerer schreiben (*Hi Patrick!*). Bei einem Brief an einen Firmenchef schreibst du besser eine formellere Anrede wie *Dear Mr Black*.

Während des Schreibens
- Um eine gute Struktur für deinen Text zu haben, gehst du am besten in der Reihenfolge deines Wortnetzes oder deiner Liste vor.
- Benutze bekannte Strukturen und Ausdrücke, z. B.: *Last Friday ... / First ... Then ... / I think ...*
- Fange nicht alle Sätze mit dem gleichen Wort an. Ersetze Namen auch mal durch *he, she* oder *it*.
- Mache deine Sätze mithilfe von Adjektiven interessanter: *great, nice ...*
- Du kannst versuchen, deine Sätze miteinander zu verbinden. Dazu kannst du diese Wörter benutzen: *and, but, because, then*.

Nach dem Schreiben
Bevor du deinen Text abgibst, lies ihn noch einmal genau durch:
- Hast du alle **Punkte der Aufgabenstellung** bearbeitet?
- Hast du deinen Text in eine **sinnvolle Reihenfolge** gebracht?
- Ist alles **verständlich**?
- Kann man deine **Schrift** gut lesen?

Completing a form

Bei diesen Aufgaben sollst du bei allen Punkten etwas eintragen.
Schreibe **keine** vollständigen Sätze.

6 **In London**

You have arrived at a hotel in London.

 Complete the form with your information.

Welcome to "Young Generation London"	
First name:	Last name:

Gender: ☐ male ☐ female	Date of birth:	Place of birth:

Address:	Email:

Nationality:	Telephone number:

Arrival date: *4 April*	Departure date: *6 April*

Single room: ✓	Double room: ☐	Breakfast: ✓

Signature:		

Answering an email

> Wenn du eine E-Mail beantworten sollst, musst du folgende inhaltliche Punkte beachten:
> - Anrede (*Hi, Hello, Dear ...*)
> - Begrüßung (*Thank you for ..., How are you?, It was nice to hear from you ...*)
> - Beantwortung der gestellten Fragen (*I would like to answer your questions ...*)
> - eine persönliche Nachricht (*I must tell you about ...*)
> - Beenden der E-Mail (*See you, Love ...*)

7 Back home

Mike visited his aunt and uncle in Australia. Now he is back home in England.

 a) Read the email.

> Dear Mike,
> Greetings from Australia!
> It was nice to have you here. We hope you enjoyed your stay and that we could show you some interesting places. How was your flight? How is the weather in England? And how is your family?
> Love,
> Uncle George and Aunt Lynn

 b) Write a "Thank you"-email from Mike and answer the questions. Write about 40–50 words.

> _____
> _____
> _____
> _____
> _____
> _____
> _____

Writing an email

8 My "after school" holiday trip

You want to go on a holiday trip after finishing school.
Your grandparents will send you the money for your trip.

Plan it!

a) Collect ideas for your holiday trip. Make a word web.

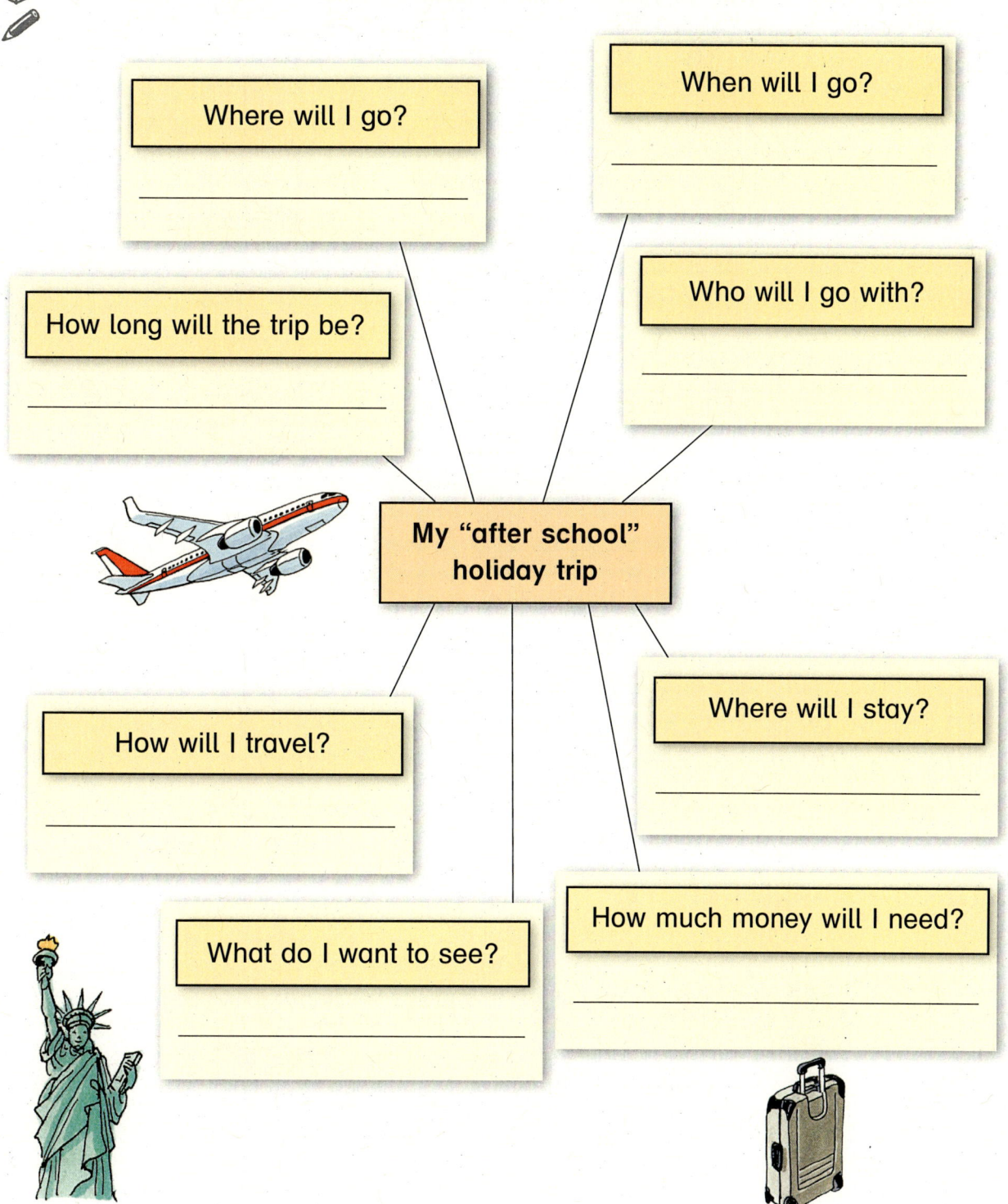

When will I go?

Where will I go?

Who will I go with?

How long will the trip be?

My "after school" holiday trip

Where will I stay?

How will I travel?

How much money will I need?

What do I want to see?

Do it!

a) Write an email to your grandparents and tell them about your holiday plans. Write about 60–80 words. Use your word web for ideas.

Denke bei deiner E-Mail an folgende Punkte:

- Anrede
- Einleitungssatz oder -frage
- Klare und genaue Informationen zu deinen Urlaubsplänen
- eventuell noch eine persönliche Nachricht
- Beenden der E-Mail
- Dein Name

Check it!

b) Read your email.
Check if everything is OK.

Achte auf die Rechtschreibung, den Schreibstil und ob du alle Kriterien für eine gute E-Mail berücksichtigt hast.

Mediation 🇬🇧🇩🇪

Diese Tipps helfen dir beim Vermitteln zwischen Englisch und Deutsch:

Manchmal kommst du in Situationen, in denen du zwischen Deutsch und Englisch vermitteln sollst. Das passiert immer, wenn du auf Personen triffst, die kein Englisch oder kein Deutsch verstehen. So musst du manchmal **englische Schilder erklären** oder **bei Gesprächen dolmetschen**.

Beim Sprachmitteln solltest du Folgendes beachten:
Sprachmitteln ist keine Übersetzung.
Übersetze also **nicht Wort für Wort**, sondern gib nur den **Sinn** wieder. Das kannst du gut in deinen eigenen Worten machen.
Du solltest aber die wichtigsten Informationen (z. B. Namen und Zahlen) nicht vergessen. Versuche immer, **einfache und kurze Sätze** zu bilden.

Da du in solchen Situationen meist kein Wörterbuch zur Hand hast, kannst du **unbekannte Wörter mit anderen Wörtern umschreiben**. Hauptsache, dein Gegenüber versteht dich.

Talking about signs

> Bei diesen Aufgaben sollst du die wichtigsten Informationen von englischen Schildern ins Deutsche übertragen. Schaue dir jeweils den Bildhintergrund an. Er hilft dir beim Verstehen der Schilder.

9 English signs

Look at the signs. Explain what they mean in German.

1 2 3

Talking about flyers

Lies dir die deutschen Fragen genau durch. Suche dann die Informationen im Flyer. Diese Aufgabe sollst du mündlich bearbeiten. Denke bei dieser Aufgabe daran, nicht Wort für Wort zu übersetzen, sondern nur das Wichtigste zu nennen.

10 An English flyer

Look at the flyer. Answer the questions in German.

Lyceum Theatre
21 Wellington Street
London, WC2E 7RQ

Performance dates:
Tuesday – Saturday
at 7.30 pm,
Wednesday, Saturday
& Sunday at 2.30 pm

Buy tickets online:
www.thelionkinginlondon.co.uk
or call 0845 321 6012

How to get there:
Take the tube to Covent Garden or Temple
or go by bus (number 168)

An welchen Tagen wird das Musical aufgeführt?

Wann beginnt die Vorstellung?

Wo kann ich die Tickets buchen?

Wie ist die Adresse des Theaters?

Mit welcher Buslinie kann ich zum Theater fahren?

Helping out in a conversation

Bei diesen Aufgaben sollst du schriftlich arbeiten. Hier sollst du zwischen einem englischsprachigen Kellner und einer Freundin vermitteln, die kein Englisch spricht. Dabei solltest du nicht Wort für Wort übersetzen. Schreibe kurze Sätze. Unbekannte Wörter kannst du in deinen eigenen Worten umschreiben.

11 At a restaurant

Read the dialogue. Then write down sentences in English and German.

1 Hello. Can I get you something to drink?

Der Kellner fragt …

2 Ich hätte gern eine Limonade.

She'd like a …

3 OK. What would you like to eat?

4 Ich hätte gern einen Salat.

5 Kann ich bitte zahlen?

6 Yes, of course. That's £12, please.

Speaking

Diese Tipps helfen dir beim Englischsprechen:

Es gibt zwei Formen des Sprechens. Den Monolog, bei dem du allein sprichst
(z. B. bei einer Präsentation) und den Dialog, bei dem mindestens zwei Personen
miteinander sprechen. Das Sprechen auf Englisch ist viel einfacher,
wenn du einige Tipps befolgst.

Vor deiner Präsentation
- Überlege dir, was du sagen möchtest. Du kannst Stichwörter auf Karteikarten schreiben oder ein Wortnetz erstellen.
- Überlege die Reihenfolge deiner Stichpunkte.
- Es ist immer gut, ein Poster, eine digitale Präsentation o. Ä. vorzubereiten. So kannst du deinen Zuhörern genau zeigen, wovon du sprichst.
- Übe deinen Vortrag vor einem Spiegel, vor einem Freund, einer Freundin oder vor deiner Familie.

Während deiner Präsentation
- Begrüße deine Zuhörer.
- Nenne dein Thema.
- Sprich langsam, deutlich und frei. Sieh deine Zuhörerinnen und Zuhörer dabei an.
- Halte dich an die Stichwörter, die du dir notiert hast.
- Zeige deinen Zuhörern, wovon du gerade sprichst (zeige z. B. auf ein Foto auf deinem Poster).

Vor eurem Dialog
Überlege dir:
- In welcher Situation befinde ich mich?
- Welche Rolle soll ich übernehmen?
- Was will mein Gesprächspartner vermutlich erfahren?
- Was will ich sagen?

Während eures Dialoges
- Schaut euch beim Sprechen an.
- Versuche, in ganzen Sätzen zu sprechen.
- Wenn du etwas nicht verstehst, frage höflich nach, z. B. mit „Sorry, I don't understand" oder „Can you say that again, please?".
- Setze Gestik und Mimik ein.
- Fällt dir ein Wort nicht ein, versuche es zu umschreiben.

> **Tipp:** Bei einem Gespräch ist nicht nur die Sprache wichtig, sondern auch, wie man sich verhält. Lasse deinen Gesprächspartner immer ausreden.

Doing a presentation

12 **My dream job**

a) Prepare a presentation about your dream job. Make a word web first.

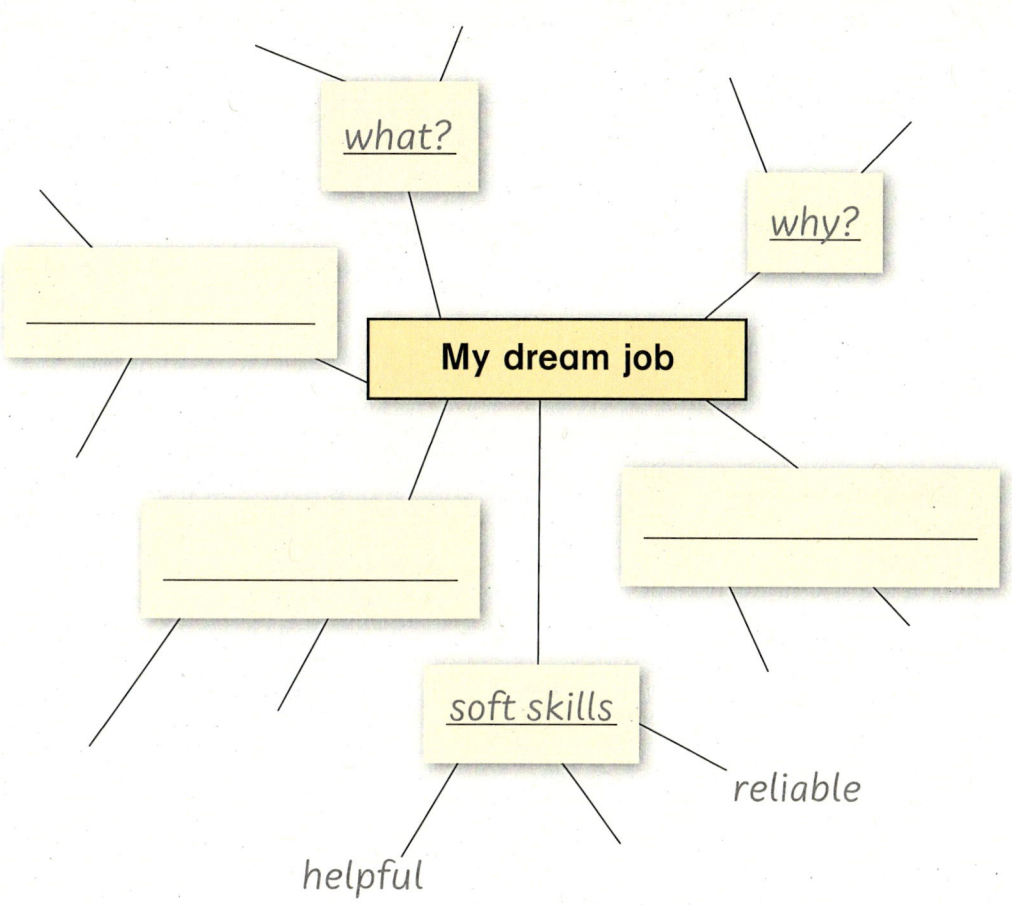

what?

why?

My dream job

soft skills

reliable

helpful

b) Do the presentation.

Hi, everyone.
Today I'd like to talk about my
dream job. I'd like to be …

Having a discussion

Bei dieser Aufgabe sollst du mit einem Partner diskutieren.
Hier sollst du dich gemeinsam mit einem Partner auf eine Auswahl einigen. Du machst Vorschläge und begründest sie. Gehe immer auf Vorschläge deines Partners ein. Stimme ihnen zu oder lehne sie ab. Benutze die Redemittel unter den Bildern.

13 **A holiday**

You and your partner want to go on holiday.

 Look at the pictures.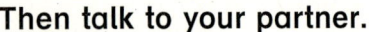
Circle the three most important things you would like to take.
Then talk to your partner.

Let's take ...

I don't agree.
We don't need ...

What about ...? • We don't need ... •
In my opinion we need ... •
Let's take ... • I agree. • I don't agree. • ...

A The perfect couple?

B
p. 154

The perfect couple?

Different cultures have different ways of finding the perfect partner for life. We spoke to Saju Chahal from India. He lives in Britain. His parents chose his wife for him. It was an arranged marriage[1]. We
5 *asked Mr Chahal what he thought about arranged marriages.*

Happily married: Saju Chahal

"In India, most people think that arranged marriages are better than love marriages[2]. A lot of people still arrange marriages for their children, even when they live here in Britain.

10 I have seen both sides. My sons got married[3] in Britain. Their wives are English, so both of them had love marriages. They are very happy. But quite often, these marriages don't last[4]. So many people get divorced[5] in Britain.

In my opinion, arranged marriages are good because they often
15 seem to last longer. My wife and I didn't expect love right from the start[6]. In most arranged marriages, love grows with time. And if there are problems, everyone tries to help: In a traditional Indian family, everyone feels responsible[7] for the marriage.

Here in Britain, people are often shocked to hear about arranged
20 marriages. Last week, a neighbour said to me that arranged marriages were old-fashioned[8] and cruel[9]. He thought that people had to marry someone they didn't like. Unfortunately, that does sometimes happen. For example, my cousin wasn't allowed to get married to the woman he loved because she was too poor. He
25 was very unhappy. His parents chose a woman for him instead. The marriage wasn't happy.

But my wife and I have had a happy marriage for over 30 years. So I think that arranged marriages are a good idea."

---

[1] arranged marriage – arrangierte Ehe
[2] love marriage – Liebesheirat
[3] got married – heiratete
[4] last – halten
[5] get divorced – sich scheiden lassen

[6] right from the start – von vornherein
[7] responsible – verantwortlich
[8] old-fashioned – altmodisch
[9] cruel – gemein

B **The journey of a cheap T-shirt**

The story of the cheap T-shirt begins in a big textile[1] company in Europe. Here, the T-shirt is designed and the managers of the company discuss how to make the T-shirt cheap. They make the price of the T-shirt just under 5 Euros.

The managers buy cotton[2] from a farmer in the US. The cotton here is cheap, because the United States government[3] pays the farmers money for it.

price now: €0.90

The cotton is made into fabrics[4]. They are sewn[5] together in a factory in Bangladesh. Mainly girls and young women work here. They don't get paid much. So the price of the T-shirt stays low.

price now: €0.908

This is Nazneen. She cuts out T-shirts. She has to do 250 T-shirts every hour. She works 10 hours a day.

Nazneen and the other women don't get paid much. Nazneen earns about €1.18 a day. That's about 15 cents an hour. So the price of the T-shirt stays low.

price now: €1.35

The manager of the factory in Bangladesh sells the T-shirts to a company in Europe. Now the T-shirts cost €1.35 each.

The T-shirts are taken from Bangladesh to Europe. They are loaded[6] onto a ship. The cost for transport is about 6 cents per T-shirt.

price now: €1.41

T-shirt € 4.99

Our cheap T-shirt has arrived in a store[7] in Europe. It costs €4.99. After taxes[8] and other costs, the textile company makes a profit[9] of about 60 cents per T-shirt. The company is making lots of money.

[1] textile – Stoff	[4] fabric – Stoff	[7] store – Geschäft
[2] cotton – Baumwolle	[5] sewn – genäht	[8] tax – Steuer
[3] government – Regierung	[6] loaded – beladen	[9] profit – Umsatz

How to talk about people

Immer wieder kommt es vor, dass du neue Leute kennenlernst.
Dann berichtest du über dich und möchtest auch einiges über den anderen
erfahren. Wie viel du dabei über dich erzählst, ist deine Entscheidung.
**Ergänze dieses Wortnetz. Du kannst damit Wörter sammeln, die dir später
bei einer mündlichen oder schriftlichen Personenbeschreibung helfen.
Suche dir anschließend einen Partner und unterhaltet euch.**

> Ihr könnt euch selbst vorstellen
> oder euch eine Person ausdenken.

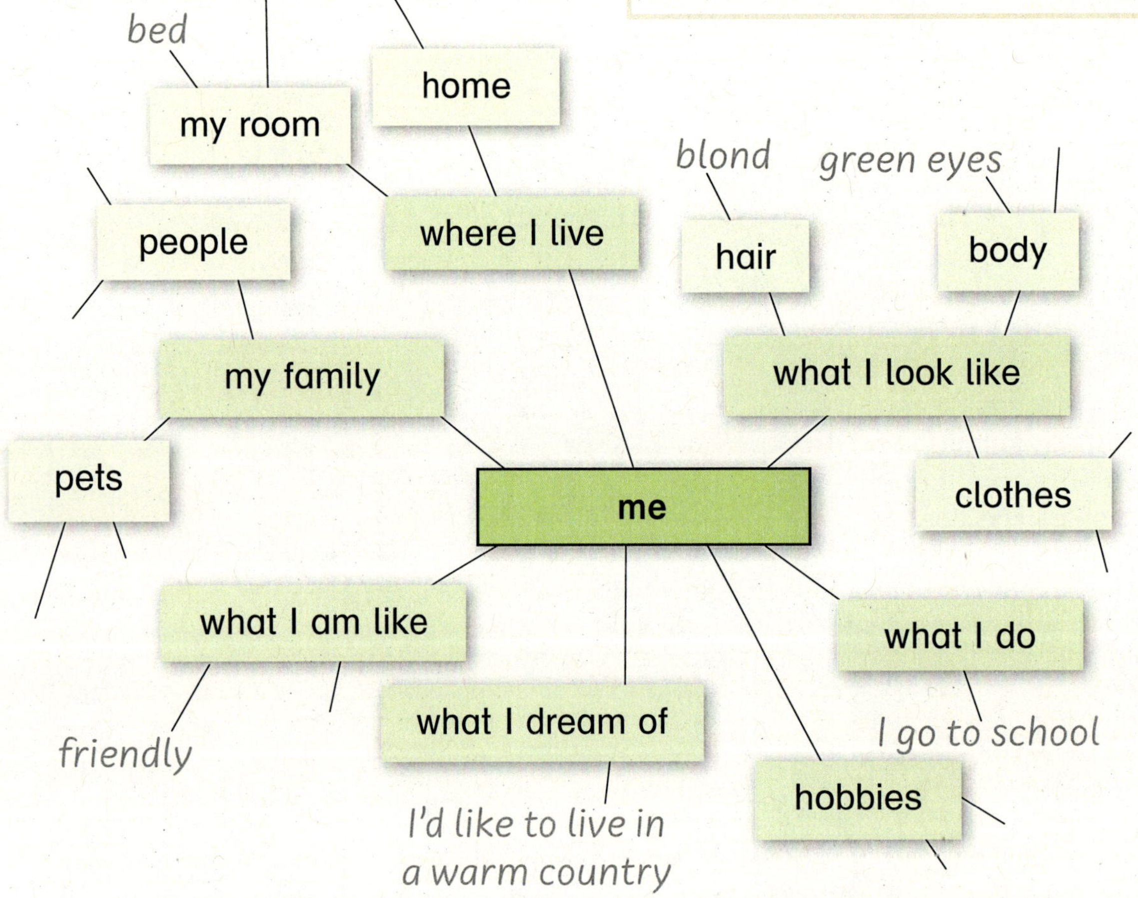

bed

my room

home

where I live

blond   *green eyes*

hair

body

people

my family

what I look like

pets

me

clothes

what I am like

what I do

friendly

what I dream of

hobbies

I go to school

*I'd like to live in
a warm country*

Hier findest du Redemittel, um dich oder andere Personen vorzustellen:

> **My name is ... • I live in ... • I live with ... • I'm good at ... • I've got ... •
> I haven't got ... • I like ... • I don't like ... • I'm interested in ... •
> My favourite ... is/are ... • I always/often/sometimes/never ...**

Mit diesen Redemitteln kannst du andere zu ihrer Person befragen:

> **What's your name? • Where do you ...? • Do you like ...? •
> What are you interested in? •
> What's your favourite ...? • What are you good at? •
> Do you always/often/sometimes ...?**

How to ask when you don't understand

Wenn du im Ausland bist, ist es manchmal schwierig zu verstehen, was andere Leute sagen. Hier sind einige Redemittel, damit du nachfragen kannst, wenn du etwas nicht richtig verstanden hast. Wenn du etwas sagen möchtest, dir aber das richtige Wort nicht einfällt, umschreibe es in einfachen Worten.

Lies dir die Beispieldialoge durch. Übe sie anschließend mit einem Partner. Ihr könnt auch eigene Ideen für die grauen Wörter einsetzen.

A: Hello. I'd like two tickets for Madam Tussauds on Saturday, please.
B: OK. We have tickets for 10 am, 11 am and 2 pm.
A: Sorry, I don't understand. Could you say that again, please?
B: Yes, of course. We have tickets …

A: Excuse me. Where is the next café?
B: There's one on Oxford Street. Do you know where that is?
A: No, I don't.
B: OK, I'll tell you the way.
A: Thank you. My English is not very good. Could you speak slowly, please?
B: Yes, of course. First, you turn …

A: Hello. How can I help you?
B: I'd like to send this postcard to Germany. But I need a … What's the word for it? You put it on letters and postcards. It's very small.
A: Oh, you mean a stamp.
B: Yes, I need a stamp for my postcard. Can I buy one here?
A: Yes, of course. That's £1.

So kannst du nachfragen, wenn du etwas nicht verstanden hast:

> Sorry, I don't understand. •
> Sorry, I don't understand what you mean. •
> Could you say that again, please? •
> My English is not very good.
> Could you speak slowly, please?

So kannst du Wörter umschreiben, wenn dir das richtige Wort nicht einfällt:

> It's made of … •
> You can use it for … •
> It's like a … • It's … •
> It can … • It has …

How to get around

Im Urlaub im Ausland musst du oft Situationen auf Englisch bewältigen.
Es kann vorkommen, dass du Tickets kaufen oder nach Informationen
fragen möchtest.

Hier sind einige Situationen abgebildet.
Spiele sie mit einem Partner nach.
Setzt eure eigenen Ideen für die grauen Wörter ein.

A: I'd like two tickets to London, please.
B: Single or return?
A: Single, please.
B: That's £25.
A: Thank you.
B: You're welcome.

A: Excuse me. When is the next train
   to Dover, please?
B: It's at 12.15.
A: Thank you. And what platform is it?
B: It's platform number 7.

A: Hello. I'd like a city map, please.
B: Here you are.
A: Thank you. How much is it?
B: It's £2.
A: Here you are. Thank you.
B: You're welcome. Bye!
A: Bye!

How to ask the way

Wenn du dich in einer fremden Stadt nicht auskennst, kann es sein,
dass du jemanden nach dem Weg fragen musst.

Lies dir den Dialog durch und zeichne den Weg in der Karte ein.
Dann übe mit einem Partner verschiedene Wegbeschreibungen.
Benutzt dabei den Stadtplan. Tauscht nach jeder Beschreibung die Rollen.

> **A:** Excuse me. How can I get to the British Museum?
> **B:** Turn left into Crown Street. Go straight on.
> Then turn right into Stanley Street and go straight on.
> It's on the left.
> **A:** Thank you.
> **B:** You're welcome.

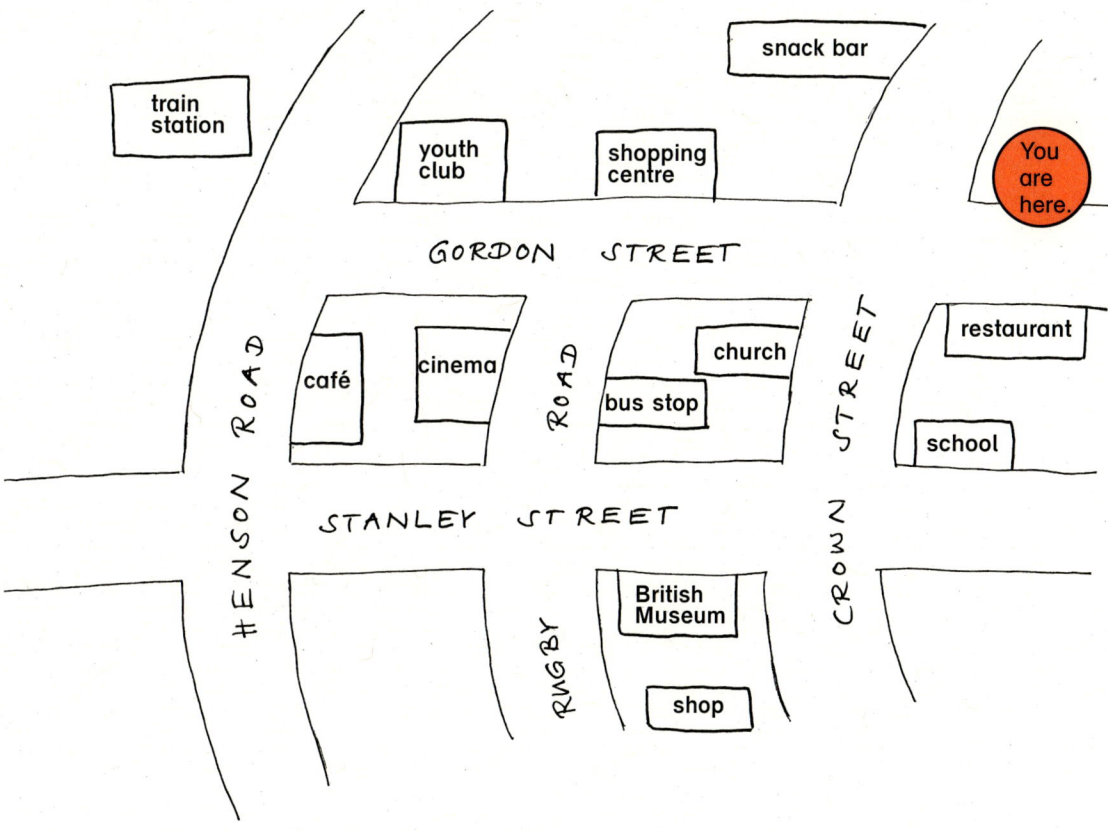

Hier findest du wichtige Redemittel für eine Wegbeschreibung und
einige Wörter für Orte in einer Stadt:

It's on the right/left. •	museum • youth club •
Turn right/left into ... •	shopping centre • cinema •
Go straight on. •	restaurant • snack bar •
It's next to ...	church • train station

How to go shopping

Wenn du im Ausland etwas kaufen oder sogar über den Preis verhandeln möchtest, dann gibt es einige Sätze, die für dich nützlich sein können.
Lies dir die Beispieldialoge durch.
Versuche anschließend, die Dialoge mit einem Partner zu lesen oder sie vorzuspielen. Die grauen Wörter könnt ihr durch eigene Ideen ersetzen.

At the market
A: Hello. How can I help you?
B: How much is this book?
A: It's £8.
B: That's too expensive for me.
A: OK. Let's say £6.
B: OK. I'll take it. Here you are.
A: Thank you, bye!
B: Bye!

In a shop
A: Hello. How can I help you?
B: I'd like to buy a T-shirt.
A: What about this one?
B: Yes, I like it. I'll try it on.
A: No, that's too big for you.
   I'll bring you a smaller one.
   What do you think now?
B: I like it. How much is it?
A: That's £15.
B: That's cheap. I'll take it.

Hier findest du einige Redemittel und Fragen, die du stellen kannst:

I'd like to buy ... •
That's too expensive. •
That's cheap. • I like it. •
I don't like it. • I'll take it.

How much ...? •
Do you have a smaller/bigger one? •
Do you have it in a different colour? •
Can I try this on, please?

How to order a meal

Wenn du auf Englisch etwas zu essen bestellen möchtest,
ist es nützlich, wenn du einige Sätze und Fragen kennst.
Probiere es mit einem Partner aus.
Spielt eine Situation in einem Restaurant nach.
Anstelle der grauen Wörter könnt ihr eigene Ideen nutzen.

> Welcome to Harper's restaurant.

> Hello. A table for one, please.

> OK. Here's the menu.

> Thank you.

> Can I get you something to drink?

> I'll have a lemonade, please.

> What would you like to eat?

> I'd like the pasta, please.

> Here is your pasta. Enjoy your meal!

> I'd like to pay, please.

> That's £14, please.

> Here you are.

> Thank you. Have a nice day.

> Thanks. Bye!

Hier findest du einige nützliche Wörter:

lemonade • coffee • orange juice • tea • water • milk • hot chocolate	pizza • salad • steak • hamburger • sandwich • hot dog • pasta

● Das muss ich noch üben.
● Ich mache noch Fehler.
● Kein Problem!

Liebe Schülerin, lieber Schüler,

auf den folgenden Seiten findest du sechs Portfolio-Fragebögen, zu jedem *Theme* einen. Jedes Mal, wenn ihr ein *Theme* fertig bearbeitet habt, füllst du einen Fragebogen aus. So kannst du feststellen, was du schon kannst.

Das geht so: Sieh dir z. B. den folgenden Satz an.
Überlege, wie gut du das kannst, was dort beschrieben ist:

○ **Ich kann ein Bild beschreiben.**
(→ Seite 22)

Vor jedem Satz steht ein Kreis: ○
Darunter steht die Seite,
auf der es eine Aufgabe dazu gibt:
(→ Seite 22)

Wenn du meinst, dass du das Beschriebene
schon richtig gut kannst,
dann male den Kreis grün aus: ●

Du bist dir noch nicht ganz sicher?
Dann male den Kreis gelb aus: ●

Wenn du noch große Schwierigkeiten hast,
dann male den Kreis rot aus: ●

Und jetzt: Viel Spaß!

1 Growing Up

Love and marriage

○ Ich kann verstehen, wenn jemand über seine Probleme spricht.
(→ Seite 14)

○ Ich kann einen schwierigen Text lesen und den Inhalt erschließen, ohne jedes Wort verstehen zu müssen.
(→ Seite 15)

○ Ich kann mir einen Text anhören und die wichtigsten Informationen herausfiltern.
(→ Seite 17)

○ Ich kann Dialogteile in die richtigen Reihenfolge bringen und den Dialog mit einem Partner vortragen.
(→ Seite 18, 19)

Teenage pregnancy

○ Ich kann einen Text lesen und wichtige Informationen darin unterstreichen.
(→ Seite 20, 21)

○ Ich kann ein Bild beschreiben.
(→ Seite 22)

○ Ich kann einem englischen Diagramm Informationen entnehmen.
(→ Seite 23)

○ Ich kann ein Filmposter erstellen und der Klasse präsentieren.
(→ Seite 24, 25)

2 Making it on your own

The start of something new

○ **Ich kann ein Gedicht lesen und verstehen.**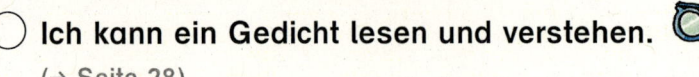
(→ Seite 28)

○ **Ich kann verstehen, wenn jemand über seine Zukunftspläne spricht.**
(→ Seite 30)

○ **Ich kann Berichte über das Thema Arbeit lesen und verstehen.**
(→ Seite 32, 33)

○ **Ich kann andere nach ihren Zukunftsplänen fragen.**
(→ Seite 34)

Bad conditions

○ **Ich kann Sätze zu den passenden Bildern zuordnen.**
(→ Seite 35)

○ **Ich kann mir einen Dialog anhören und verstehen.**
(→ Seite 36)

○ **Ich kann deutsche Fragen über ein englisches Diagramm beantworten.**
(→ Seite 38)

○ **Ich kann ein T-Shirt mit einer wichtigen Aussage entwerfen.**
(→ Seite 41)

3 South Africa – The Rainbow Nation

Sights and attractions

○ **Ich kann anhand eines Dialoges Bildunterschriften prüfen.**
(→ Seite 44)

○ **Ich kann auf Deutsch über eine englische Bordkarte sprechen.**
(→ Seite 45)

○ **Ich kann eine Reisebroschüre lesen und verstehen.**
(→ Seite 46, 47)

○ **Ich kann mir ein Telefongespräch anhören und wichtige Informationen herausfiltern.**
(→ Seite 48, 49)

Past and present

○ **Ich kann Fragen zu einem Sachtext beantworten.**
(→ Seite 51)

○ **Ich kann Texte über die Gegenwart und die Vergangenheit von Südafrika lesen und verstehen.**
(→ Seite 53)

○ **Ich kann auf Deutsch über den Inhalt englischer Texte sprechen.**
(→ Seite 53)

○ **Ich kann ein Poster über Südafrika erstellen und präsentieren.**
(→ Seite 54, 55)

4 Changes and challenges

Natural disasters

○ Ich kann mithilfe gesprochener Texte
Bildunterschriften zu Bildern zuordnen.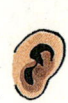
(→ Seite 58)

○ Ich kann ein einfaches Rätsel
zum Thema Naturkatastrophen lösen.
(→ Seite 60)

○ Ich kann beim Hören einen Lückentext ausfüllen.
(→ Seite 61)

○ Ich kann wichtige Informationen eines
englischen Textes auf Deutsch wiedergeben.
(→ Seite 62)

Keeping in touch

○ Ich kann sagen, was man im Internet
machen und nicht machen kann.
(→ Seite 65)

○ Ich kann eine Umfrage führen.
(→ Seite 66)

○ Ich kann einen Flyer lesen und verstehen,
der Aussagen zur Sicherheit im Internet macht.
(→ Seite 69)

○ Ich kann mein eigenes Profil erstellen
und sagen, was ich im Internet veröffentlichen würde.
(→ Seite 71)

Auf den folgenden Seiten kannst du noch einmal nachschlagen, wie du etwas sagen kannst.

1

So kannst du auf Englisch **über dich selbst** Auskunft geben:

My name is Rajiv.

I am sixteen years old.

I have got a sister. / **I've got** a sister.

I haven't got a brother.

2

So kannst du **über eine andere Person** Auskunft geben:

 **His** name **is** Ben.

He **is** from England.

He has got two sisters.

He has milk for breakfast.

 **Her** name **is** Vicky.

She is sixteen years old.

She likes bungee jumping.

She wants to go surfing.

Weißt du noch? Bei einem **Tier** sagt man *it*:

It likes meat.

3

So sagst du, ob du etwas **magst**:

🙂 I **like** pizza.

🙁 I **don't like** yoghurt.

So **fragst** du, ob jemand etwas **mag**:

Do you **like** salad? – Yes, I do. / No, I don't.

So **fragst** du, was jemand **besonders gerne mag**:

What is your **favourite** snack?

4

So kannst du ausdrücken, **wie** du etwas **findest**:

I think the film was **great** / **good** / **OK** / **boring**.

I think the music was **too slow** / **too fast** / **interesting** / **funny**.

So kannst du sagen, was du **gerne tun würdest**:

I'd **like to** see Table Mountain.

5

So sagst du, **wie häufig** du etwas tust:

I **always** clean my room.

I **usually** hoover.

I **often** look after my brother.

I **sometimes** cook.

I **never** clean the kitchen.

5

So sagst du, **wie lange** du etwas tust.

I listen to music **for 20 minutes**.

So **fragst** du, **wie lange** jemand etwas tut:

How long do you listen to music **for**?

6

So sagst du, dass jemand etwas **nicht tun kann**:

I **can't** often go swimming. / She **can't** often go swimming.

So drückst du aus, dass jemand etwas **nicht hat**:

I **haven't got** a computer. / He **hasn't got** a computer.

So sagst du, dass jemand etwas **nicht tut** (oder z. B. **nicht mag** oder **bekommt**):

I **don't** like the music. / She **doesn't** eat meat.

7

Wenn du erzählen möchtest, **was eine andere Person über sich selbst gesagt hat**, musst du einige Wörter verändern:

I am …	–	**He / She** is …
My parents …	–	**His / Her** parents …
We lived …	–	**They** lived …
Our house …	–	**Their** house …
… for **me**.	–	… for **him / her**.

8

So kannst du ausdrücken, dass etwas **in der Zukunft passieren wird** (z. B. morgen, nächste Woche oder nächstes Jahr):

> I **will** start my new job in September.

> You **will** be seventeen next year.

So kürzt du *will* ab:

> There'**ll** be more robots in 800 years.

Achtung: *Will* nicht verwechseln mit dem deutschen „will" (= wollen). Das englische *I will* heißt auf Deutsch „ich werde".

9

So kannst du erzählen, was schon **passiert ist**:

Meist hängt man an das Verb einfach ein **-ed**. Das kennst du schon!

> Natasha watch**ed** TV.

Es gibt aber auch Verben, für die du die Verbform lernen musst.

Gillian **was** alone.	–	Gillian **war** allein.
Charlie **got** a present.	–	Charlie **bekam** ein Geschenk.
They **went** shopping.	–	Sie **gingen** einkaufen.
Rajiv **didn't** like the burger.	–	Rajiv **mochte** den Burger **nicht**.

Fragen stellst du so:

> **Did** you go online yesterday?

10

So **fragst** du, ob jemand schon einmal etwas getan oder
probiert hat:

> **Have** you ever play**ed** rugby? – Yes, I have / No, I haven't.
> **Have** you ever watch**ed** a tennis match on TV? –
> Yes, I have. / No, I haven't.

Manchmal musst du aber das Verb verändern:

> **Have** you ever **tried** bungee jumping? – Yes, I have. / No, I haven't.

11

„Was wäre, wenn …?"
Diese Frage kannst du auch auf Englisch stellen.
Dort gibt es die sogenannten *if-clauses*. Sie werden auch
Konditionalsätze oder Bedingungssätze genannt.
Ist etwas nicht ganz unwahrscheinlich, benutzt du im **Satzteil mit if**
die **einfache Gegenwart** (*simple present*).
Im zweiten Satzteil verwendest du **will** oder **'ll**.

> If I ever **go** to Cape Town, I **will** go to Robben Island.
> If she **finds** his address, she**'ll** send him a postcard.

12

Wenn du nicht ganz sicher bist, wie etwas sein wird,
dann sagt man das im Englischen so:

> **I think** Kevin will leave Northern Ireland.
> **I guess** his mum will be very sad.
> **Maybe** Stacey will go with Kevin.

13

So kannst du Wörter im Englischen **abkürzen**, wenn du sprichst oder z. B. eine E-Mail schreibst:

I **am** = I'm
I **have** got = I've got
I **will** = I'll
I **would** = I'd

you **are** = you're
they **are** = they're

they **have** = they've

it **is** = it's
what **is** = what's
that **is** = that's
there **is** = there's

let **us** = let's

14

So kannst du Fragen stellen:

What are your plans for the holidays?
When would you like to come?
Where do you work?
Who is that?
Why do you live in England?
How will you get there?
How long would you like to stay?
How much do you earn?

A

English	German	Example
a / an	ein(e); pro	**a** girl / **an** animal
abbreviation	Abkürzung	
have an abortion	abtreiben lassen	
about	über; ungefähr	
accept	akzeptieren	
accepting	Annahme; Akzeptieren	
across	(hin)über	
actor / actress	Schauspieler(in)	
after	nach; nachdem	
afternoon	Nachmittag	
again	wieder, noch einmal	
against	gegen	
age	Alter	at the **age** of – im Alter von
(two years) ago	vor (zwei Jahren)	
agree	zustimmen, einer Meinung sein	I don't **agree**. – Ich stimme nicht zu.
airport	Flughafen	
be alive	am Leben sein	
all	ganz; alle(s)	**all** day – den ganzen Tag
all in one	alles in einem	
allow	erlauben	
(not) be allowed to	(nicht) dürfen	
already	schon	
also	auch	
always	immer	
amazing	erstaunlich, toll	
and	und	
animal	Tier	
annoying	ärgerlich	
another	noch ein(e)	**another** piece – noch ein Stück
answering	Beantworten	
antique	Antiquität	
any	(irgend)ein	
anything	irgendetwas	
apartheid	Apartheid, Rassentrennung	
apprenticeship	Ausbildung	
are / aren't	bist, sind, seid / bist nicht, sind nicht, seid nicht	
area	Bereich, Zone	
argument	Streit; Argument	
around	um	
arrival	Ankunft	
arrive	ankommen	I **arrived** – ich kam an
art	Kunst	
as	als; wie	
assistant	Helfer; Mitarbeiter	
at	in; an; um; bei	

Athens	Athen
aunt	Tante
author	Autor(in)
Australia	Australien

B

bad	schlecht	
bag	Tasche	
baggage	Gepäck	
bake	backen	
baker	Bäcker(in)	
bakery	Bäckerei	1 **bakery** – 2 bakeries
Bangladesh	Bangladesch	
barricade	Barrikade	
basement	Keller	
be	sein	I **was** – ich war
be from	herkommen	
beach	Strand	
because	weil	**because** of – wegen
become	werden	I **became** – ich wurde
bed	Bett	
been	gewesen	
beer	Bier	
before	vorher; bevor	
begin	anfangen; beginnen	I **began** – ich begann
bench	Sitzbank	
believe	glauben	
best	beste(r, s); am besten	
better	besser	
between	zwischen	
bigger	größer	
birth	Geburt	
birthday	Geburtstag	Happy **birthday**! – Alles Gute zum Geburtstag!
black	schwarz	
blew	wehte	
boarding pass	Bordkarte	
boarding time	Einsteigezeit	
body	Körper	
bomb	Bombe	
book	Buch	
booking reference	Buchungsnummer	
bored	gelangweilt	
boring	langweilig	
born	geboren	I was **born** – ich wurde geboren
both	beide	
bother sb	jdn stören	
bought	kaufte(n)	
boy	Junge	
bread	Brot	
breakfast	Frühstück	

brick	Ziegel	
bridge	Brücke	
bring	(mit)bringen	I **brought** – ich brachte (mit)
Britain	Großbritannien	
British	britisch	
broken	kaputt	
brother	Bruder	
build	bauen	
builder	Bauarbeiter(in)	
bully	mobben	
bullied	gemobbt	
bus stop	Bushaltestelle	
but	aber; außer	
buy	kaufen	I **bought** – ich kaufte
by	bis; von; mit	
bye	Tschüss	

C

cable car	Seilbahn	
call	anrufen; rufen; nennen; Anruf	I **called** – ich rief an
came	kam(en)	
can / can't	können / nicht können	I **can** swim – Ich kann schwimmen
candle	Kerze	
Cape Town	Kapstadt	
car	Auto	by **car** – mit dem Auto
car technician	Autotechniker(in)	
carpet	Teppich	
carry	tragen	
celebrate	feiern	
challenge	Herausforderung	
change	(ver)ändern; Veränderung	
Changing of the Guard	Wachwechsel	
chapter	Kapitel	
(main / favourite) character	(Haupt- / Lieblings) charakter	
chat	chatten; Unterhaltung	
cheap	billig, preiswert	
cheaper	billiger	
cheer	jubeln, Jubel	
child(ren)	Kind(er)	
child labour	Kinderarbeit	
choice	Wahl	
chores	Haushaltspflichten	
chorus	Refrain	
church	Kirche	
cinema	Kino	to go to the **cinema** – ins Kino gehen
city	(Groß)stadt	
city centre	Stadtmitte; Innenstadt	
class	(Eisenbahn-)Klasse	

classmate	Mitschüler(in)
clean	sauber machen; sauber
cleaning	Saubermachen
clock	Uhr
close	nah
closed	gesperrt; geschlossen
clothes	Kleider, Kleidung
club	Verein
coffee	Kaffee
colleague	Kollege / Kollegin
colour	Farbe
come	kommen
comment	Kommentar
company	Firma, Unternehmen
completing	Vervollständigen
completion	Vervollständigung
con	Kontra
condition	Zustand; Bedingung
contact	kontaktieren; Kontakt
conversation	Gespräch
cook	Koch / Köchin; kochen
cooking	Kochen
cool	kühl
correct	richtig; korrigieren
cotton	Baumwolle
could	könnte(n); konnte(n)
country	Land
couple	(Ehe)paar
language course	Sprachkurs
cousin	Cousin(e)
cover (up)	etwas verdecken
craftsmen	Handwerker
crossword	Kreuzworträtsel
cut (out)	(aus)schneiden
cyberbullying	Mobbing im Internet

Seitliche Beispiele:

It is 7 o'clock. – Es ist 7 Uhr.

textile **company** – Textilfirma

correct answer – richtige Antwort

1 **country** – 2 countries

D

dancing	Tanzen
dangerous	gefährlich
date	Datum; Verabredung
dating	Partnersuche
day	Tag
dead	tot
deadly	tödlich
dear	liebe(r, s) (z. B. in Briefen)
decide	(sich) entscheiden
decorate	schmücken, dekorieren
delicious	köstlich, lecker
democratically	demokratisch
departure	Abfahrt

once a **day** – einmal pro Tag

description	Beschreibung
designer label	Modelabel
destroy	zerstören
detect	aufspüren; erkennen
dictionary	Wörterbuch
did / didn't	tat / tat nicht
different	verschieden(e)
difficult	schwierig
dirty	schmutzig, dreckig
disaster	Katastrophe
discover	entdecken
discriminate against	benachteiligen; diskriminieren
discuss	besprechen
have a discussion	eine Diskussion führen
dishwasher	Geschirrspülmaschine
distracted	abgelenkt
do / don't	tun / nicht tun, machen / nicht machen
doctor	Arzt / Ärztin
doing	Tun, Machen
door	Tür
double room	Doppelzimmer
down	unten; herunter
download	herunterladen
dream	Traum, Traum-; träumen
dress	Kleid
drink	Getränk; trinken
drinking	Trinken
drinking water	Trinkwasser
drought	Dürre
drum	Trommel
dry	trocken
during	während
duty (pl. duties)	Pflichten, Aufgaben

dictionary entry – Wörterbucheintrag

natural **disaster** – Naturkatastrophe

What are you **doing**? – Was machst du?

I **drank** – ich trank

E

each	jede(r, s)
earn	verdienen
earthquake	Erdbeben
East, east	Osten, östlich
eat	essen
economy	Wirtschaft
education	Ausbildung
egg	Ei
elect	wählen
elected	gewählt
else	sonst
empire	Imperium, Weltreich

I **ate** – ich aß

empty	leeren
end, ending	enden, aufhören; Ende
English	Englisch; englisch
the English	Engländer(innen)
enjoy	genießen
enough	genug
equal	gleich
equipment	Ausrüstung, Ausstattung
even	sogar
evening	Abend
ever	jemals
every	jede(r, s)
everyone	alle; jeder
everything	alles
example	Beispiel
Excuse me.	Entschuldigen Sie bitte.
expect	erwarten
expensive	teuer
experience	Erfahrung; Erlebnis
eye	Auge

every week – jede Woche

for **example** – zum Beispiel

in my **experience** –
   nach meiner Erfahrung

F

face	Gesicht
factory	Fabrik
fair trade	fair gehandelt; fairer Handel
fall	fallen
false	falsch
famous	berühmt
farmer	Landwirt(in)
fast	schnell
father	Vater
favourite	Lieblings-
fear	Befürchtung; Furcht
feel	(sich) fühlen
feelings	Gefühle
female	weiblich
festival	Fest
a few	ein paar
fight (against / for)	kämpfen (gegen / um)
file	Datei
finding	Finden
finish	beenden; Ziel
finished	beendete(n); fertig, beendet
finishing	Beenden
fireworks	Feuerwerk
first	erste(r, s); zuerst
flat	Wohnung
flea market	Flohmarkt
flight	Flug

I **fell** – ich fiel

faster – schneller

a few minutes –
   ein paar Minuten

flood	Überschwemmung
follow	folgen
food	Essen
football	Fußball
football player	Fußballspieler
for	für; um
for example	zum Beispiel, beispielsweise
for life	lebenslänglich
foreign	ausländisch
forget	vergessen
form	bilden; Formular
France	Frankreich
free	frei
freedom fighter	Freiheitskämpfer(in)
friend	Freund(in)
make friends	Freunde machen
friendly	freundlich
friendship	Freundschaft
from	von; aus
in front of	vor
fruit	Frucht, Obst
full	voll, ganz
(have) fun	Spaß (haben)
funny	lustig, witzig
(piece of) furniture	Möbel(stück)
future	Zukunft; zukünftig

I **forgot** – ich vergaß

I am **from** Germany. –
Ich komme aus
Deutschland.

G

game	Spiel
gardener	Gärtner(in)
gender	Geschlecht
German	Deutsch; deutsch
the Germans	die Deutschen
Germany	Deutschland
get	bekommen; kommen; holen; bringen; werden
get around in sth	mit etw klarkommen
get lost	sich verlaufen
get on well with sb	sich mit jdm gut verstehen
get under sth	sich unterstellen
girl	Mädchen
girlfriend	Freundin; Partnerin
give	schenken; geben
give away	weggeben
give up for adoption	zur Adoption freigeben
go	gehen; fahren
go away	weggehen
go by	vorbeigehen
go on	weitergehen
go out	ausgehen

I speak German. –
Ich spreche Deutsch.

I **got** – ich bekam

I **went** – ich ging

good	gut	
be good at sth	etw gut können	I **am good at** singing. –
		Ich kann gut singen.
goodbye	Tschüss, auf Wiedersehen	
got	erhielt(en), bekam(en)	
grandparents	Großeltern	
great	großartig, toll; groß	
Great Britain	Großbritannien	
green	grün	
greetings	Grüße	
grid	Tabelle	
ground	(Erd)boden	
group	Gruppe	work in **groups** –
grow	wachsen	in Gruppen arbeiten
growing up	erwachsen werden	
guard	Wachposten	
guess	vermuten; raten	
guest	Gast	
city guide	Stadtführer(in)	

H

had	hatte(n)	
had to	musste(n)	
hair	Haar(e)	
hairdresser	Friseur(in)	
half	Hälfte	
happen	geschehen, passieren	it **happened** – es geschah
happy / happily	glücklich	
harbour	Hafen	
have / haven't	haben; essen; trinken /	
	nicht haben; nicht essen;	
	nicht trinken	
have got	haben	I **have got** a dog. –
		Ich habe einen Hund.
have to	müssen	
having	Haben	
he	er	
head	Kopf	
heading	Überschrift	
hear	hören	
held	gehalten	
help	Hilfe; helfen	Can you **help** me? –
helpful	hilfsbereit	Kannst du mir helfen?
helping out	Aushelfen	
her	ihr; sie	
here	hier; hierher	
Here you are.	Da hast du es.	
high school	Sekundarschule	
him	ihn; ihm	
himself	sich selbst	
his	sein(e)	

history	Geschichte
hit	treffen; schlagen
hold a speech	eine Rede halten
holiday	Urlaub
holidays	Ferien
home	Zuhause
home town	Heimatstadt
work from home	Home Office machen
homeless	heimatlos, obdachlos
homework	Hausaufgaben
hoover	staubsaugen
hope	hoffen
host family	Gastfamilie
hot	heiß
hot chocolate	heiße Schokolade
hour	Stunde
house	Haus
housekeeper	Haushalter / Haushälterin
how	wie
how much	wieviel
human rights	Menschenrechte
hut	Hütte

I **held a speech**. –
   Ich hielt eine Rede.

I **hope** so. – Ich hoffe es.

How are you? – Wie geht
   es dir?

I

I	ich
idea	Idee
if	wenn, falls; ob
ill	krank
important	wichtig
impression	Eindruck
in	in, im; auf
India	Indien
Indian	Inder(in); indisch
inhabitants	Einwohner
injured	verletzt
inside	innen
instead	stattdessen
interest	Interesse, Hobby
be interested in	sich für etw interessieren
interesting	interessant
into	in
invent	erfinden
invention	Erfindung
ironing	Bügeln
is / isn't	ist / ist nicht
island	Insel
it	es
its	sein(e); ihr(e)

J

jacket	Jacke
jewellery	Schmuck
join	beitreten, eintreten
joiner	Schreiner
journey	Reise
juice	Saft
jumping	Springen
just	gerade; genau; nur; einfach

go on a **journey** –
  auf eine Reise gehen

K

keep	behalten
keep in touch (with)	in Kontakt bleiben (mit)
keyword	Schlüsselwort
get killed	getötet werden
killer	mörderisch, tödlich
kind	Art, Sorte
kingdom	Königreich
kitchen	Küche
know	kennen; wissen
get to know	kennenlernen

I **kept** – ich behielt

kind of music – Art von
  Musik

L

label	beschriften; Etikett
child labour	Kinderarbeit
land	Boden, Festland
language	Sprache
the largest	der / die / das größte
at last	endlich
last	letzte(r, s); (an)dauern
late	(zu) spät
later (on)	später
lead to	führen zu
leading	führend
learn	lernen
at least	wenigstens, mindestens
leave (from)	verlassen; weggehen; abfahren
left	links; verließ(en)
lemonade	Limonade
lesson	Unterricht
let	lassen; ließ(en)
Let's ...	Lass(t) uns ...; Lass(t) uns ...!
letter	Brief; Buchstabe
lie	lügen
life	Leben
life imprisonment	lebenslange Haft
lift off	abheben

it **led to** – es führte zu

Let's work together! – Lass
  uns zusammen arbeiten!

light	Licht
light up	anzünden
like	mögen; wie
lion	Löwe
listener	Zuhörer(in)
listening	Hören
little	klein; wenig
live	leben, wohnen
load	Ladung; einräumen
local	örtlich, einheimisch
long	lang
(any) longer	(night) länger
look after	aufpassen auf
look for	suchen
look like	aussehen wie
look up	nachschlagen
get lost	sich verlaufen
lose	verlieren
a lot of, lots of	viel(e)
loud	laut
love	Liebe; lieben, sehr gern mögen; viele Grüße (z.B. in Briefen); Liebes-
fall in love	sich verlieben
low	niedrig
lucky	glücklich, Glück haben

I **like** chocolate. –
   Ich mag Schokolade.

love story –
   Liebesgeschichte

M

made	machte
be made of sth	aus etw hergestellt sein
magazine	Zeitschrift
make it	es schaffen
make money	Geld verdienen
make to do sth	Miene machen, etw zu tun
making	Machen
male	männlich
many	viele
map	Karte
market	Markt
marriage	Ehe
marry	heiraten
match	Übereinstimmung; Spiel
matching	zusammenpassend; Zuordnen
me	mir, mich
meal	Mahlzeit
mean	bedeuten; meinen; gemein
measure	messen
measurement	Messungen

I **meant** – ich meinte

meat	Fleisch	
mediation	Sprachmittlung	
meet	(sich) treffen	We **met** – wir trafen (uns)
meeting friends	Freunde treffen	
member	Mitglied	
men	Männer	
menu	Speisekarte	
message	Nachricht, Botschaft	
met	traf(en)	
meteorologist	Meteorologe	
mid-	mittel-	
middle	Mitte	
milk	Milch	
missing	fehlend	
mix (up)	vermischen, verrühren	
mobile phone	Handy	
moment	Moment, Augenblick	
money	Geld	
month	Monat	
more	mehr; zusätzlich(e)	**more** questions – mehr Fragen
morning	Morgen	
most	der / die / das meiste	
mother	Mutter	
mountain	Berg	
move	sich bewegen	
mow the lawn	den Rasen mähen	
Mr	Herr	
Mrs	Frau	
Ms	Frau	
much	viel	
multiple choice	Mahrfachauswahl	
mum	Mama	
music	Musik	
must	müssen	
my	mein(e)	
myself	mich; ich selbst	

N

name	Name; nennen	
nation	Staat, Nation	
nationality	Staatsangehörigkeit	
natural	natürlich	
need	brauchen; müssen	I **need** help! –
neighbour	Nachbar(in)	Ich brauche Hilfe!
the Netherlands	die Niederlande	
never	nie	
new	neu	
next	nächste(r, s)	
nice / nicely	schön, nett; gut	
no	nein; kein(e)	

Nobel Peace Prize	Friedensnobelpreis
non-smoking	nichtrauchend
non-whites	Farbige
normally	normalerweise
North, north	Norden, nördlich
Northern Ireland	Nordirland
not	nicht
nothing	nichts
now	nun, jetzt
number	Zahl, Nummer

O

ocean	Ozean, Meer	
of	von	
offer	anbieten; Angebot	
office	Büro	
often	oft	
old	alt	I am 15 years **old**. – Ich bin 15 Jahre alt.
the Olympic Games	die Olypmischen Spiele	
on	auf; an; in; am	
on time	pünktlich	
one day	eines Tages	
only	nur	
onto	auf	
open	öffnen	
opinion	Meinung	
or	oder	
orange juice	Orangensaft	
order	Reihenfolge; bestellen	
other(s)	andere(r, s)	
our	unsere(r, s)	
out	aus; hinaus; heraus	
outside	draußen	
over	über	
own	eigene(r, s)	my **own** room – mein eigenes Zimmer

P

page	Seite	
painter	Maler(in)	
palace	Palast	
paper	Papier	
paragraph	Absatz	
parents	Eltern	
park ranger	Parkaufseher(in)	
part	Teil	in **parts** of South Africa – in Teilen Südafrikas
partner	Partner(in)	
passenger	Passagier(in)	
past	Vergangenheit	
pasta	Nudeln	
pay	bezahlen	I **paid** – ich bezahlte

peacefully	in Frieden, friedlich	
penguin	Pinguin	
people	Leute, Menschen	
per	pro	twice **per** week – zweimal pro Woche
perform	auftreten; aufführen	
performance	Aufführung	
personal	persönlich	
pet	Haustier	
phone	anrufen; Telefon	
photo	Foto	
picture	Bild, Foto	
piece	Teil, Stück	
pigeon	Taube	
place	Ort	
plan	Plan; planen	I **planned** – ich plante
plane	Flugzeug	
platform	Bahnsteig	
player	Spieler(in)	
playing	Spielen	
please	bitte	
plumber	Klempner(in)	
poem	Gedicht	
Poland	Polen	
police	Polizei	
policeman / policewoman	Polizist(in)	
polite	höflich	
political	politisch	
poor	arm	
postcard	Postkarte	
practice	Übung	
practise	üben: ausüben	I **practised** – ich übte
teenage pregnancy	Teenagerschwangerschaft	
pregnant	schwanger	
prepare	zubereiten; vorbereiten	be **prepared** – vorbereitet sein
present	Geschenk; Gegenwart	
price	Preis	
prison	Gefängnis	
pro	Pro, Für	
produce	herstellen	
pull out	herausziehen	
put	legen, stellen, setzen; kleben	

Q

queen	Königin	
question	Frage	
quickly	schnell	run **quickly** – schnell rennen
quietly	ruhig	

R

rain	Regen; regnen
rainbow	Regenbogen
reading	Lesen
ready	bereit
really	wirklich
reason	Grund
relationship	Beziehung
release	freigeben, Freigebung; veröffentlichen, Veröffentlichung
reliable	zuverlässig
repair	reparieren; Reparaturen
report	Bericht
respected	respektiert
result	Ergebnis
return	zurückkommen
return ticket	Hin- und Rückfahrkarte
right	richtig; Recht; rechts; genau, direkt
ring	klingeln
river	Fluss
room	Zimmer
rotating	rotierend
round	Runde
rule	Herrschaft; Regel
run	führen; laufen

be **ready** – bereit sein

the phone **rang** – das Telefon klang

I **ran** – ich lief

S

sad	traurig
safe	sicher
safer	sicherer
safety	Sicherheit
said	sagte(n)
salad	Salat
sausage	Wurst
saw	sah(en)
be scared	Angst haben
school	Schule
the second largest	der / die / das zweitgrößte
see	sehen
sell	verkaufen
send	schicken
sent	gesendet, geschickt
sentence	verurteilen; Satz
separate	trennen
serious	ernst

I **am scared**! – Ich habe Angst!

sentence part – Satzteil

serve	Bedienung
service	auftischen
serving	Servieren
several	einige, verschiedene
sewn	genäht
shark	Hai
she	sie
sheet	Blatt
ship	Schiff
shocked	schockiert
shop	Geschäft, Laden
shop assistant	Verkäufer(in)
go(ing) shopping	Einkaufen gehen
shopping centre	Einkaufszentrum
short	kurz
should	sollte(n)
shout	schreien, rufen
show	zeigen
radio / TV show	Radio-/Fernsehprogramm
be sick of sth	etw satthaben
side	Seite
sight	Sehenswürdigkeit
sightseeing	Besichtigung von Sehenswürdigkeiten
sign	Schild; Zeichen; Symbol
signature	Unterschrift
silly	albern, dumm
single room	Einzelzimmer
single ticket	einfache Fahrt
sister	Schwester
slow, slowly	langsam
slum	Elendsviertel
small	klein
smaller	kleiner
smoking	Rauchen
snack bar	Imbissstube
so	also; deshalb
and so on	und so weiter
social network	soziales Netzwerk
society	Gesellschaft
sold	verkaufte(n)
some	etwas; einige, ein paar
someone	jemand
something	etwas
sometimes	manchmal
son	Sohn
Sorry!	Entschuldigung!
soup	Suppe
soup kitchen	Suppenküche
the South, south	Süden, südlich

several children –
einige Kinder

I **went shopping** –
ich ging Einkaufen

walk **slowly** –
langsam gehen

South Africa	Südafrika
souvenir	Andenken
Spanish	spanisch; Spanisch
speak	sprechen, reden
speaking	Sprechen
special	besondere(r, s)
speech	Rede
spend	ausgeben; verbringen
stadium	Stadion
(go up the) stairs	Treppe (hinaufsteigen)
stamp	Briefmarke
stand (for)	stehen (für)
start	anfangen, beginnen
state	Staat
statement	Aussage
station	Bahnhof
stay	bleiben; Aufenthalt
stay away	fernbleiben
still	noch immer; trotzdem
stop	stehen bleiben; anhalten; aufhören; Halt
storm	Sturm, Gewitter
story	Geschichte
straight on	geradeaus
street	Straße
stressed out	gestresst
strong	stark
subject	Fach
successful / successfully	erfolgreich
sun	Sonne
support	Unterstützung; unterstützen
surprised	überrascht
survive	überleben
sweet	süß, niedlich

I **spoke** – ich sprach

I **stood** – ich stand

go **straight on** – geradeaus gehen

T

table	Tabelle; Tisch
take (with)	dauern; (mit)nehmen
take shelter	in Deckung gehen
talking	Sprechen
task	Aufgabe
taught	gelehrt, beigebracht
teach	unterrichten
teacher	Lehrer(in)
team	Mannschaft
tell	erzählen; sagen; feststellen
tennis player	Tennisspieler
than	als
thanks / thank you	danke

I **took shelter** – ich ging in Deckung

that	dass; der, die, das
the	der, die, das
their	ihr(e)
them	sie; ihnen
then	dann
there	dort; dorthin
there is / are ...	es gibt ..., da ist / sind ...
these	diese
they	sie (Mehrzahl)
thing	Ding, Gegenstand
think	denken, glauben
thinking	Denken
this	diese(r, s)
thought	dachte(n)
through	durch
throw	werfen
tidying	Aufräumen
time	Zeit; Mal
timetable	Fahr- / Zeitplan
title	Überschrift
to	zu; für; an; nach; bis
today	heute
together	zusammen
told	erzählte(n)
too	zu; auch
tools	Werkzeuge
top	Spitze
topic	Thema
total	Summe
touch	berühren
touch down	landen
tour	Führung
tower	Turm
town	Stadt
train	Zug
train station	Bahnhof
transport	Verkehrsmittel; Reisekosten
travel	reisen
travelling	Reisen
tree	Baum
tried	versuchte(n)
trip	Reise; Ausflug
be no trouble	kein Problem sein
true	wahr
trust	vertrauen
try	versuchen, probieren
try on	anprobieren
tube	U-Bahn
turn	abbiegen
turtle	Wasserschildkröte

from **then** on – von da an

I **threw** – ich warf

next **time** – nächstes Mal

by **train** – mit dem Zug

TV	Fernseher, Fernsehen
twice	zweimal
twin town	Partnerstadt
twister	Wirbelwind, Tornado
typical	typisch

U

the UK	Vereinigtes Königreich
uncle	Onkel
uncomfortable	unbehaglich
under	unter
understand	verstehen
unfortunately	leider
unhappy	unglücklich
unhealthy	ungesund
unskilled	ungelernt, nicht ausgebildet
up	nach oben, hinauf; hoch, oben
upload	hochladen
the USA	die Vereinigten Staaten
us	uns
use	benutzen, verbrauchen
usually	normalerweise
vegetables	Gemüse
very	sehr
view	Ansicht, Meinung; Aussicht
violent	gewalttätig
visit	besuchen
volcanic eruption	Vulkanausbruch
volunteer	Freiwillige(r); ehrenamtlich
vote	wählen

I don't **understand**. – Ich verstehe nicht.

I **used** – ich benutzte

W

wait	warten
water / waitress	Kellner / Kellnerin
(go for a) walk	gehen; Spaziergang
want	wollen
warehouse	Lager
warehouse worker	Lagerarbeiter(in)
was	war
washing	waschen
waste	verschwenden; Verschwendung
watch	beobachten, anschauen; gucken
watching	Ausschau halten
water	Wasser
waterfront	Hafergebiet, Ufer
way	Weg; Art und Weise
we	wir

I **waited** – ich wartete

wear	tragen	I **wore** – ich trug
weather	Wetter	
weather balloon	Wetterballon	
weaving machine	Webmaschine	
week	Woche	
welcome	willkommen (heißen)	
well-known	gut bekannt	
went	ging(en); fuhr(en)	
were	war(st, en, t)	
whale	Wal	
what	was	
when	wann; als; wenn	
whenever	wann auch immer	
where	wo; woher; wohin	**Where** is he? –
which	welche(r, s)	Wo ist er?
who	der / die / das; wer	
whoever	wer auch immer	
whole	ganz	
why	warum	
wildfire	Lauffeuer	
will	werden	
wing	Flügel	
wish	Wunsch	
with	mit; bei	
without	ohne	**without** help –
woman	Frau	ohne Hilfe
women	Frauen	
wonder	sich fragen	
won't = will not	werde nicht	
wood	Holz	
word web	Wortnetz	
wordbank	Wortsammlung	
work	arbeiten; funktionieren; Arbeit	I **worked** – ich arbeitete
work experience	Praktikum; Berufserfahrung	
worker	Arbeiter(in)	
working	Arbeiten	
world	Welt	
worried	besorgt	
worst	schlechteste, schlimmste	
would	würde(st, n, t)	
wouldn't = would not	würde(st, n, t) nicht	
writing	Schreiben	
wrong	falsch	
wrote	schrieb(st, en, t)	

Y

year	Jahr
yellow	gelb
yes	ja

yesterday	gestern
yet	noch nicht
you	du, dich, dir; man
you're welcome	bitte schön
young	jung
youngest	jüngste(r, s)
your	dein(e), euer
yourself	dich; du selbst
youth club	Jugendzentrum
youth hostel	Jugendherberge
youth magazine	Jugendzeitschrift

Z

zoo-keeper	Tierpfleger(in)

The days of the week

Monday

Tuesday

Wednesday

Thursday

Friday

Saturday

Sunday

The months

January

February

March

April

May

June

July

August

September

October

November

December

The seasons

spring

summer

autumn

winter

Numbers

1	one
2	two
3	three
4	four
5	five
6	six
7	seven
8	eight
9	nine

10	ten
11	eleven
12	twelve
13	thirteen
14	fourteen
15	fifteen
16	sixteen
17	seventeen
18	eighteen
19	nineteen

20	twenty
21	twenty-one
22	twenty-two
23	twenty-three
24	twenty-four
25	twenty-five
26	twenty-six
27	twenty-seven
28	twenty-eight
29	twenty-nine

30	**thirty**
31	thirty-one
…	
40	**forty**
41	forty-one
…	
50	**fifty**
51	fifty-one
…	
60	**sixty**
61	sixty-one
…	
70	**seventy**
71	seventy-one
…	
80	**eighty**
81	eighty-one
…	
90	**ninety**
91	ninety-one
…	
100	**one hundred**
101	one hundred and one
…	
1000	**one thousand**
1001	one thousand and one
…	
1010	one thousand and ten
…	
1100	one thousand one hundred
1101	one thousand one hundred and one
…	

Tracktliste der CD

Discovering Europe

1.	1	Teenagers in Europe (Sophie)
2.	1	Teenagers in Europe (Marcel)
3.	1	Teenagers in Europe (Marika)
4.	3	Typical German?
5.	4	Travelling to Oxford

1 Growing up

Love and marriage

6.	1	At the bus stop
7.	2	Kevin and Sadie
8.	3	The story goes on
9.	4	Kevin's plans

Teenage pregnancy

| 10. | 8 | The story |
| 11. | 11 | On the radio |

2 Making it on your own

The start of something new

12.	1	The start of something new
13.	2	Job bingo
14.	3	Future plans
15.	5	Jessica
16.	6	Torge

Bad conditions

| 17. | 9 | Human rights |

3 South Africa

Sights and attractions

18.	1 a)	Impressions of South Africa
19.	1 c)	Impressions of South Africa
20.	4	Sightseeing in Cape Town
21.	5	Isabel's tour

Past and present

| 22. | 9 | Nelson Mandela |
| 23. | 10 | Gimme hope Jo'anna |

4 Changes and challenges

Natural disasters

24.	1	Natural disasters
25.	4	A survival story
26.	5 b)	A tornado warning
27.	5 d)	A tornado warning
28.	6	Warning systems

Keeping in touch

| 29. | 9 | On the phone |
| 30. | 11 | Talking on the radio |

5 Exam practice

31.	1	Leonie
32.	2	Train to London (Rashid)
33.	2	Train to London (Charlotte)
34.	3	A family photo

Reading is fun

| 35. | B | The journey of a cheap T-shirt |

Audio-CD:

westermann GRUPPE

Listening texts are produced by John Green and recorded by Tim Woolf, London. Speakers: Sophie Aldred, Brian Bowles, DeNica Fairman, John Green, John Hasler, Harriet Kershaw, Gregg Lowe, Rachael Miller, Claire Morgan, Richard Pearce, Nigel Pilkington.

Song:

23 "Gimme hope Jo'anna", Text und Musik: Eddy Grant, © 1988 by Greenheart Music LTD. EMI Music Publishing Germany GmbH, Berlin, Parlophone (LC 00299)

Bildquellen:

Cover: Dirk Schmidt/dsphotos.de

|A1PIX - Your Photo Today, Ottobrunn: /SAT 78.3. |action press - die bildstelle, Hamburg: Rex Features Ltd. 65.3. |adpic Bildagentur, Köln: Neudert 6.2, 6.2, 7.2. |Alamy Stock Photo (RMB), Abingdon/Oxfordshire: 14.1, 91.1; Itani Images 71.3; Segre, Alex 96.1; © The Art Gallery Collection 52.1. |alimdi.net, Deisenhofen: Strenske, Bettina 78.1. |Art Explosion, Calabasas, CA: 6.3. |Averil Grieve, North Fitzroy: 85.2. |Colourbox.com, Odense: 16.3. |ddp images GmbH, Hamburg: Seth Rossman/US Navy/UPI 60.4. |Deutsche Bahn AG, Frankfurt: 10.1. |dreamstime.com, Brentwood: Kaphoto 79.1. |dsphotos.de / Dirk Schmidt Photography, Hamburg: Titel. |fotolia.com, New York: 31.3, 57.2, 64.5, 70.1; Coloures-pic 40.1; gilitukha 60.3; Grinvalds, Kaspars 65.4; ikonoklast_hh 31.1; Jung, Michael 67.1; Khvost 40.3; maconga 45.1, 45.2, 45.3; Minerva Studio 60.1; Monkey Business 96.2; Popov, Andrey 65.2; rsooll 60.2; Taylor, Stuart 44.2; Winzer, Barbara 71.1. |Getty Images, München: AFP 35.6; Bambu Productions 58.1; Dianne Christie 50.3; Fraser Hall 46.4; Per-Anders Petterson 52.2; © Ricky Leaver/LOOP IMAGES 3.1; © Warren Faidley 57.1, 58.4. |Hammersen-Schiffner, Bettina, Braunschweig: 85.1. |Hild, Claudia, Angelburg: 70.2. |iStockphoto.com, Calgary: 64.6; (c) mikanaka 40.2; ajr_images 39.1; kadmy 65.1; monkeybusinessimages 73.2; Ridofranz 67.2; Roger Jegg 15.1; SlobodanMiljevic 60.5; Sunnybeach 78.2; valeriebarry 53.1, 53.2; visual7 16.2. |Lee Gone Publications, Hove: from the How To Be British Collection 8.1. |Maciej Dakowicz Photography: 36.2. |mauritius images GmbH, Mittenwald: age 35.4; imagebroker/jspix 44.3; imagebroker/Niehoff, Ulrich 35.5; imagebroker/Stephan Gabriel 27.1, 32.1, 32.1; Peter Enzinger 73.1; Prisma 35.1; Wolfgang Weinhäupl 6.4, 6.4, 7.3. |OKAPIA KG - Michael Grzimek & Co., Frankfurt/M.: 63.1. |Picture-Alliance GmbH, Frankfurt/M.: akg-images 35.3; Augenklick / KUNZ 50.2; Design Pics 71.5; Design Pics/LJM Photo 71.2; dpa 50.1, 58.2, 58.5; dpa / DB Kathrin Streckenbach 33.1; dpa / epa 27.2, 35.2, 43.3, 50.4, 51.2, 51.2; dpa / epa AFP Casella 58.3; dpa / Larry W. Smith 59.1; dpa/dpaweb/Haid, Rolf 10.2; dpa/Hörhager, Felix 31.2; empics / David Davies 12.1, 43.1, 46.2, 46.2; epa Hrusa 51.1; The Advertising Archives 86.1, 86.2; ZB/Lander, Andreas 65.6. |plainpicture, Hamburg: Gorilla 71.4; Matzen, Anna 6.1, 6.1, 7.1. |Shutterstock.com, New York: 96.3; Africa Studio 64.4; Jorg Hackemann 15.2, 17.1; Kneschke, Robert 65.5; Peter Titmuss 44.1; Rainer Lesniewski 16.1; StanislavBeloglazov 36.3. |stock.adobe.com, Dublin: 43.2, 44.4, 44.5, 44.6, 46.1, 46.3, 46.3. |Süddeutsche Zeitung - Photo, München: SSPL/Science Museum 64.2. |TV-yesterday, München: Weber, Wolfgang Maria 64.3. |ullstein bild, Berlin: 64.1; Westend61/Kopp, Florian 36.1. |UNICEF Deutschland, Köln: 38.2; UNI40322/Nesbitt 38.1. |vario images, Bonn: Kiefer, Stefan 31.4. |wikimedia.commons: 10.3. |World Vision Deutschland e.V., Friedrichsdorf: Mark Nonkes 40.4.

Textquellen:

15 Excerpt from "Across the Barricades", Joan Lingard (Hamish Hamilton, 1972) © Joan Lingard, 1972, p. 48-49. Reproduced by permission of Penguin Books Ltd.

52 "Gimme hope Jo'anna", Text und Musik: Eddy Grant, © 1988 by Greenheart Music LTD. EMI Music Publishing Germany GmbH, Berlin

World Map

Scale
0
1000
2000
3000
4000
5000
km

Abbreviations:
AL — Albania
BIH — Bosnia and Herzegowina
CH — Switzerland
CZ — Czechia
H — Hungary
HR — Croatia
L — Luxembourg
MD — Moldova
MNE — Montenegro
MZ — Macedonia
SK — Slovakia
SLO — Slovenia
UAE — United Arab Emirates

Oceans
Pacific Ocean
Atlantic Ocean
Arctic Ocean
Indian Ocean
Southern Ocean
Pacific Ocean

North America
NORTH AMERICA
Canada
United States of America
Mexico
Guatemala
El Salvador
Belize
Honduras
Nicaragua
Costa Rica
Panama
Caribbean Islands
Greenland
Iceland

South America
SOUTH AMERICA
Colombia
Ecuador
Venezuela
Guyana
Suriname
Peru
Brazil
Bolivia
Chile
Paraguay
Argentina
Uruguay

Europe
EUROPE
Norway
Sweden
Finland
United Kingdom
Ireland
Nether-lands
Belgium
France
Germany
Denmark
Poland
Estonia
Latvia
Lithuania
Belarus
Ukraine
CH
Austria
H
Italy
CZ
SK
AL
Greece
Romania
Bulgaria
Serbia
BIH
HR
MNE
Mz
MD
Portugal
Spain
Malta
Cyprus

Africa
AFRICA
Morocco
Algeria
Tunisia
Libya
Egypt
Western Sahara / Sahara
Mauritania
Mali
Niger
Chad
Sudan
Eritrea
Senegal
Gambia
Guinea-Bissau
Guinea
Sierra Leone
Liberia
Ivory Coast
Burkina Faso
Ghana
Togo
Benin
Nigeria
Cameroon
Cape Verde
São Tomé and Principe
Equatorial Guinea
Gabon
Congo
Democratic Republic of the Congo
Central African Republic
South Sudan
Ethiopia
Somalia
Djibouti
Uganda
Kenya
Rwanda
Burundi
Tanzania
Angola
Zambia
Malawi
Mozam-bique
Zimbabwe
Botswana
Namibia
South Africa
Swaziland
Lesotho
Madagascar
Comoros
Seychelles
Mauritius
Maldives

Asia
ASIA
Russia
Turkey
Georgia
Armenia
Azer-baijan
Syria
Lebanon
Israel
Jordan
Iraq
Iran
Kuwait
Bahrain
Qatar
UAE
Oman
Yemen
Saudi Arabia
Kazakhstan
Uzbekistan
Turkmenistan
Tajikistan
Kyrgyzstan
Afghanistan
Pakistan
India
Nepal
Bhutan
Bangladesh
Sri Lanka
Mongolia
China
North Korea
South Korea
Japan
Myanmar
Thailand
Laos
Vietnam
Cambodia
Malaysia
Brunei
Singapore
Indonesia
Philippines
Timor-Leste
Pacific Islands

Australia
AUSTRALIA
Australia
New Zealand
Papua New Guinea

Antarctica
ANTARCTICA

16.0w
© westermann

CAMDEN
MARKET
6

Diesterweg

westermann

IV A social network profile

> Du musst nicht alles ausfüllen. Denk darüber nach, was du im Internet veröffentlichen würdest.

News (230)▼ Favourites▼

Name:
_____
_____

Age:
_____

Gender: _____

Birthday: _____

Home town: _____

Relationship status: _____

Email: _____

Looking for: _____

Political views: _____

Personal information

Hobbies: _____

_____

Interests: _____

Favourite music: _____

Favourite TV shows: _____

Favourite films: _____

Favourite books: _____

About me: _____

CAMDEN
MARKET
6

westermann

Isabel's tour

CAMDEN MARKET 6

II Job bingo

Spielregeln

1. Wählt einen Bingo-Master. Die übrigen Schüler sind Bingo-Spieler.
2. Die Bingo-Spieler schreiben die Berufe durcheinander in ihr Bingo-Feld.
3. Der Bingo-Master liest die Berufsbeschreibungen **durcheinander** vor. Die Bingo-Spieler nennen den Beruf und kreisen ihn in ihrem Bingo-Feld ein.
4. Wer zuerst vier Wörter in einer Reihe, in einer Spalte oder diagonal eingekreist hat, ruft laut „Bingo!" und gewinnt das Spiel.

> Diese Karte mit Berufsbeschreibungen ist für den Bingo-Master.

> He or she repairs cars.

> sells things in a shop • works with plants and trees •
> cooks food in a restaurant • bakes bread •
> paints rooms and houses • works at school •
> works on a farm • plays football • works in a warehouse •
> washes and cuts hair • works outside and has to be strong •
> repairs cars • works in National Parks • looks after animals •
> plays tennis • looks after ill people

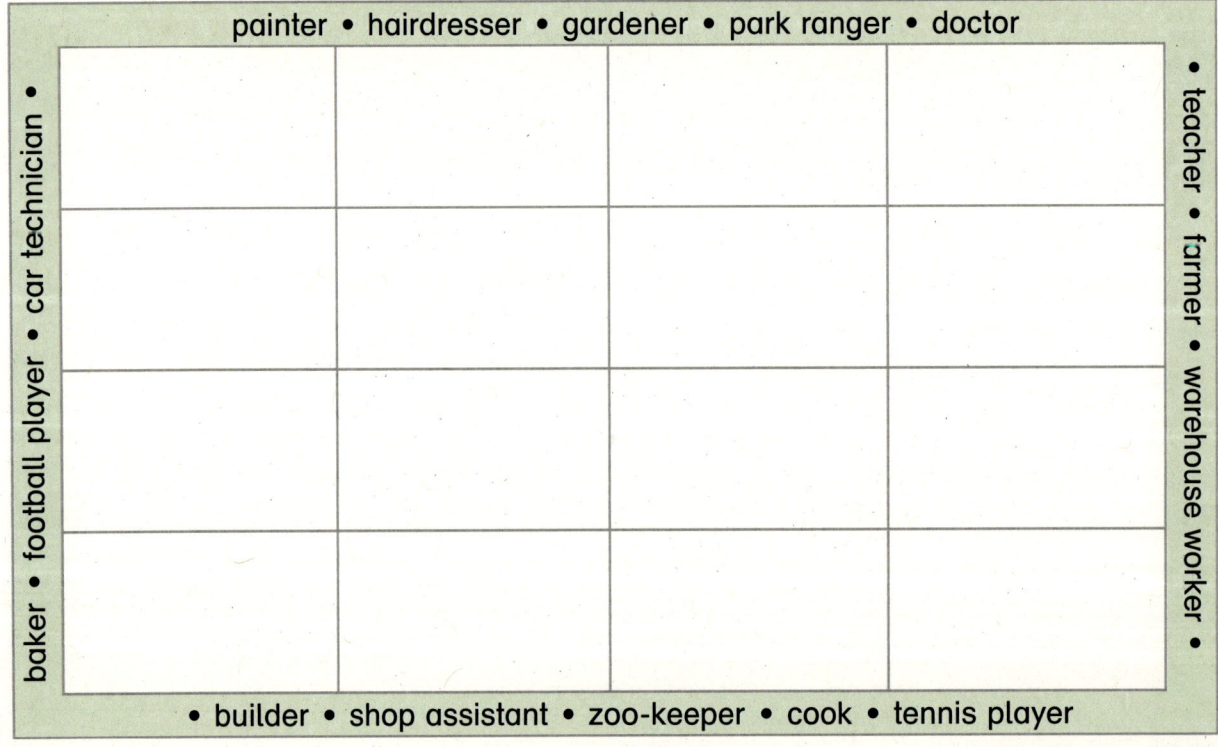

CAMDEN MARKET

6

Diesterweg

westermann

I A dialogue

> Hi, Mum.
> Listen, I want to tell you something.

> Sadie wants to stay in Belfast. I have to go now.
> The ship will leave soon. Bye, Mum.

> I am sick of bombs and people getting killed.
> I've got to go away. I can't stay here any longer.

> I'm going to Liverpool.
> I'll write to you when I get there.

> Hi, Kevin.
> What is it? Are you alright?

> You can't just run away, Kevin!
> Where will you go?

> No, Kevin, come back!
> Please don't leave! Kevin!

> But who are you going with?
> Are you going with that girl, Sadie?